40 Days
& Nights

Your Healing Journey to
Freedom and Purpose

Julz Muya

Website: www.mymentor.life/juliamuya
Email: julzmuya@gmail.com
Facebook: www.facebook.com/julzmuya
Instagram: @julzmuya

First Published in United States of America
by Julia Muya 2020
ISBN: 978-1-7361178-0-4

For my son, Josiah-Peter

In loving memory of
Mia Tomada Doerksen and Faith Ngunju

Contents

i

Foreword

The number 40 signifies new life, fresh growth, and transformation. It often characterizes a time of preparation for a calling or accompanies the movement of an actively deepening faith.

The rain of the Great Flood lasted 40 days and nights.

Moses fasted 40 days and nights to prepare himself to receive the Law.

The Israelites wandered the desert for 40 years after fleeing Egypt.

The prophet Elijah walked 40 days and nights to Mount Horeb.

Jesus fasted 40 days and nights to prepare for his public ministry.

I wrote this book in 2020 when I was 40 years old.

Testimonial

Andiswa Madolwana

Nearly two years ago, I found myself in a place where I did not know whether I was coming or going. Stuck in a foreign land with just my thoughts and feelings of failure, I knew I needed help. With the guidance of the Holy Spirit, I reached out to Julz, who wasted no time in taking my hand and leading me away from the dark abyss I was slowly making my home.

The Bible says it is better for two to walk together than it is to walk alone, for if one stumbles and falls, the other will pick him up. I have seen this word come to life over the last two years. Walking in accountability has helped me deal with and face even the parts of myself that I had been intentionally running away from. Through discipleship, God has released and delivered me from years of shame and guilt that I had accepted as my portion, as part of who I am.

I know that I might have reached this freedom at some point, but it would certainly have taken much longer. I probably would have caused myself more harm before eventually turning back to the right track. But having someone walk the tough road with me, holding my hand in prayer and allowing herself to cry with me through the difficult moments, has redirected my life.

For years I struggled with being vulnerable—even with myself. But since Julz empowered me to open up, let go, and surrender to God, I have been redeemed. Through discipleship, I have seen my identity regained and my voice restored. I now know and truly believe that I can live a life of purpose, that the failures and disappointments along the way were a wake-up call. Although my trials were a part of my journey that I might have struggled ever to come to terms with or embrace on my own, Julz's biblical guidance made both possible.

I stand victorious today, fully healed and restored, solely thanks to the ministry of one-on-one discipleship. I have learned to stop hiding from myself. Julz reminded me to trust in God completely, even when it seems not to make any sense, because God will always reveal himself and bring breakthrough for me!

Preface

The year 2020 has been a rough one for me, as it has for everyone. In a span of just three months, cancer took my niece, my marriage fell apart, and I lost my job. All this happened in the midst of a pandemic that has drastically altered the geography of human life and interaction. However, I have found that suffering incites spiritual awakening and a hunger for truth. God is moving and speaking to me in ways I have never before experienced—or noticed. I recognize that, without God, I am feeble, blind, and wretched. There is absolutely nothing good in me apart from Christ. Every word in this book reflects the transformation God has begun in my heart. He chose me, in all my selfish immaturity, to share his gospel—a fact which proves he can use anything and anyone for the sake of his glory.

If you want to find freedom and purpose, ask God to further his kingdom through you. This book will not only launch you toward your own healing journey but also equip you to support others through theirs. The gospel spreads exponentially. Think of COVID-19, which started with just one person in China. Within months, that first little virus became a global pandemic. Likewise, if just one brave soul shares the Word of God with a friend, salvation will spread to the rest of the world. You don't need to bellow from the spotlighted stage of a big church to make an impact. The Holy

Spirit gives you influence wherever you are. Begin by discipling one or two. If they do the same, it's only a matter of months before the message spreads to thousands.

This model of one-on-one discipleship was originally taught by Jesus. Preparing new believers for the challenges ahead, it has proven to be a successful and efficient way of sharing the gospel with every tribe, tongue, and nation. Discipleship requires vulnerability and authenticity. You must be willing to extend your hand to people navigating uncharted, rocky terrain. By working with them through their pain, you will see firsthand how God mends the broken heart and heals the wounded soul. You will become a vessel of his transformation. Such personal investment comprises some of the most rewarding yet understated work you'll ever do. It is unglamorous, void of accolade and fame. But it is guaranteed to leave a lasting legacy of Christ on Earth.

Introduction

God's healing journey can be long and complex, a topic difficult to cover thoroughly in one book. This guide functions as both a conversation starter to get your feet moving and a roadmap to steady your path.

At times, you may disagree with my point of view. That is okay. Like the Bereans in Acts 17:11, you should be discerning in all things. At times, I miss the mark or fail to align with experts in the field. But it's my individual experience with God that inspired me to write this book. For the next 40 days, take time to self-reflect. Search for the truth that will set you free and fill you with purpose. If you have wandered from God, I pray you will reconnect with him and develop a close relationship. Separated into five parts, this book mirrors the steps I took though my own healing journey:

Part I – Knowing Your Identity

The feeling that comes after a breakup or the death of a loved one is awful. It's a sense of having lost yourself, like a piece of you has gone missing and is nowhere to be found. The same sensation occurs on a spiritual level when we lose touch with God. Our identity and self-esteem are rooted in our relationship with him. This section of the book will help you dig into your history and determine where things went wrong. By applying biblical truth to situations that became spiritual hurdles, you can break free from the dysfunctional patterns keeping you chained to the past. The less worthy you feel, the more likely you are to blame others for your perceived inferiority. Inner healing does not come from self-love. Rather, it comes from focusing on God's immeasurable love for you and expanding your measurable love for him. The foundation of your worth is Christ.

Part II – Knowing God

The best way to recognize counterfeit money is by studying authentic bills. Likewise, when we spend time studying God's character, we can better discern his voice and recognize the enemy's deception. The secret to discovering your purpose is first knowing the author and giver of your life. If you don't know God, you cannot know what he has in store for you. He is the source of your supply. This section will familiarize you with the heart and character of your Creator.

Part III – Knowing Your Enemy

If you want a faith that can withstand fire, you must be equipped to recognize and combat your enemy, the devil. This section will expose the lies Satan commonly uses to delude the human mind, blinding us to both God's identity and our own. In the beginning, everything was good—until the devil deceived Eve and ushered sin into the world. Although no longer a snake, Satan never misses a chance to deceive us about who God is and, thus, who we are.

Part IV – Knowing the Truth

This section will teach you to be good Bereans, or analysts of truth. We are living in the last days when many false prophets will emerge, preaching messages that are easy on the ears but lead to destruction. Every time I listen to a sermon, I question its biblical validity no matter who is preaching. I implore you to do the same. If you read something in this book that seems contrary to God's Word, highlight it and do your research. This book is meant to inspire you to question your beliefs and seek the truth for yourself.

Part V – Knowing Your Purpose

God gives his people immense purpose and wonderful callings— but discovering those can be a process. This final section will discuss the importance of Jesus' instruction to go out, spread the gospel, and set captives free. I realized God's purpose for my life only after he had healed me. It was then that he opened my eyes to the true fulfillment that comes from answering his call. Everyone has a unique role in the kingdom of God, but all roles boil down to service. There are many opportunities to love this hurting world. Think about the people Jesus highlighted: orphans, widows, the poor, the sick, the voiceless, and most importantly, the spiritually lost. What's your role?

At the end of each chapter, I pose a series of questions that should inspire you to write in your journal. If you're not a fan of writing, don't stress. The questions can still help you contemplate the state of your heart and relationship with God. As you read, ask God to reveal his truth. This book cannot change your life. But it will point you to the person who can. Only Jesus has the power to transform human hearts. I am just a vessel he can use to ignite a fire within you and initiate the healing you've been longing for.

PART I

Knowing Your Identity

Day 1

The Gist of Gender

6-19

Ephesians 5:21-33

The more I get to know God, the more I understand who I am in him. The more I draw near to God, the more I appreciate my femininity and unique role in this world as a woman. In the past, my desire for self-reliance led me to misplace my female identity. Before I got married, I was in control of every aspect of my life. Threatened by the prospect of having my power stripped away, I gravitated toward men who were passive. Exhaustion, stress, and bitterness filled my heart as I adopted a biblically masculine role. By misplacing my identity as a woman, I walked myself right into a dysfunctional marriage. The repercussions of that decision were a wakeup call. I had lost myself. Broken, confused, I asked my Creator to remind me who I am and the role he designed me for. And God did. He restored my true identity, revealing the two major symptoms of one that is misplaced.

The essence of sin is self-reliance (control) and self-exaltation (pride). It rears its head first in rebellion against God and then in exploitation of others. While secular society often uses the term "toxic" to shame men and women for not conforming to cultural norms, the Bible does address abuse of power in both genders. In biblical terms, toxic masculinity could be defined as the selfish effort

2

of a man to dominate, subdue, and exploit women for his own evil desires. Likewise, toxic femininity could be defined as the selfish effort of a woman to dominate, subdue, and exploit men for her own evil desires. The difference between the two lies chiefly in the hardwired weaknesses of each gender. When sin drives a woman, she uses her sexuality to overpower men; when sin drives a man, he uses his physical strength to subjugate women. The battle for control is rooted in humanity's sinful nature and fueled by a lack of submission to God's will.

The Bible instructs believers to submit to one another out of reverence for Christ (Ephesians 4:1-6, 5:21). Jesus himself set the perfect example of submission when he came to Earth as a man. Instead of appealing to his equality with God, he humbled himself as a servant and gave his life willingly for us (Philippians 2:6-11).

Single, married, separated, divorced, widowed—it doesn't matter. God-given femininity remains the same no matter the status. Your identity is grounded in submission to Christ. Your role is to fulfill the purposes he's called you to. A godly woman embraces her design, speaks wisely, lives confidently, and trusts God's promise of reward (Proverbs 31:25-26, 30). If you are single and in search of a partner, remember this: A godly man rejects passivity, accepts responsibility, leads courageously, and trusts God's promise of reward. He gladly obeys the Lord, protects and provides for his family, and loves his one wife (1 Timothy 3:1-7).

Although I misplaced my identity, I found it in Christ. You can too. No longer intimidated by traits I once considered weak, I am rebuilding my home on a solid foundation. The home is the domain in which feminine virtue blossoms and shines. My duty when mentoring a younger woman is to encourage her in purity, kindness, wisdom, modesty, and gentle strength. I must help her discover what it means to be called as a daughter of God and teach her to be a godly wife and mother (Titus 2:3-5). Together, we will firmly establish her identity in Christ. In other words, godly women are to train younger women to be just that: *women* of God.

Do any of your behaviors suggest that you might meet the Bible's definition of toxic femininity? What shame, fear, or insecurity lies at the root of your misplaced identity? Read Proverbs 31 and bask in the truth that God designed you beautifully for great purpose. Ask him to reveal any habits keeping you from biblical womanhood. How can you address them together?

Day 2

The Culture of Self

Romans 1:18-32

We live in a culture that glorifies self. Instead of looking to Christ for healing, society turns inward. Self-actualization, self-love, self-help, self-healing, self-reliance—none of these secular solutions work. My healing began when I quit navel-gazing. As I prioritized the needs of others and relied on God to fulfill me, Christ replaced me as the center of my life. The contrast between inner focus and upward focus was stark. How vain my old life had been! Well into adulthood, I'd functioned like a child vying for validation. Curious about cultural remedies to selfishness, I started reading up on the characteristics of a narcissist. I was shocked to see myself painted in the list of traits. *Was* I a narcissist? The world might jump to diagnose me—but the Bible offers a different perspective.

That said, let's talk about potential for growth. Can narcissists, both clinically- and self-diagnosed, change? Yes. There is power in the cross of the resurrected Christ to break anyone free from any stronghold (Romans 6:1-3). Nothing is impossible with God (Matthew 19:25-26, Luke 1:37). The Apostle Paul said "it is God who works in you to will and to act in order to fulfill his good purpose"

(Philippians 2:13). We must all go through the process of sanctification to become mature Christians ready to serve God.

The traits of an immature person are almost identical to those that describe a narcissist. Naturally, every human is plagued with a handful of flaws to work on. But we must be careful to protect our hearts from those who have given themselves over to their sin (Proverbs 4:23; Ephesians 4:19). If antisocial traits or ungodly behaviors abound in a man you're dating, don't expect marriage to magically mature him. True change comes from surrender to God (2 Corinthians 5:17).

The first step toward maturity is recognizing the signs of immaturity. Here are the 10 I've found most common:

- ❖ **Lack of empathy**. Immature people struggle to understand or share the feelings of others. The Bible warns that the last days will be filled with godlessness and self-idolatry (2 Timothy 3:2). The more our faith matures, the better we become at elevating and empathizing with our neighbors.

- ❖ **Misplaced anger:** Instead of treating past challenges as opportunities to learn, immature people lash out. Their anger may manifest as simmering resentment or explosive outbursts. Because they are unwilling to face their history, they pour their frustrations onto their closest loved ones (Psalm 37:8).

- ❖ **Victimization.** Instead of taking responsibility for their own shortcomings, immature people blame others. They point fingers, justifying wrong actions with accusations that *he made* *me do it* or *she pushed me to the edge—I had no choice* (Proverbs 19:9).

❖ **Instant gratification.** Immature people sacrifice long-term wisdom for short-term pleasure. This myopia can result in financial ruin, reckless sexual behavior, and criminality. Acting on impulse, they barge head-first into temptation with little or no thought about the consequences (Proverbs 14:16).

❖ **Egocentrism.** Like toddlers, immature people are trapped within themselves. Blind to other points of view, they do only what seems best for them. Mature people see the big picture. Open to multiple perspectives, they temper their actions by considering the wisdom and needs of others (James 3:17).

❖ **Hostility.** When confronted or contradicted, immature people default to personal attack. Hostility can manifest as emotional abuse (sarcasm, character assassination, silent treatment, gaslighting) or escalate to physical abuse (Titus 3:1-2).

❖ **Deception and manipulation.** Immature people tell lies even when honesty would cost them nothing. Hiding their insecurities behind a mask of fabrication, they will do anything to maintain a good appearance (Galatians 1:10). Mature people are secure in their identity and do not fear authenticity.

❖ **Blurred boundaries.** Fudging one line and toeing another, immature people sabotage healthy relationships. Though their offenses are often inadvertent, such people do not grasp the importance of respecting boundaries. This disregard for others sometimes ends in an immature person's becoming either a victim or perpetrator of abuse (Luke 6:31).

❖ **Superficiality.** Immature people lack depth. Instead of valuing character, they chase attractiveness, intelligence, wealth, status, charisma, and power—anything that will meet their basest needs (1 Samuel 16:7). That's why close relationships with immature people leave mature people feeling used.

❖ **Arrogance.** Convinced they know it all, immature people are deaf to feedback. Puffed up with pride, they have neither room nor desire for personal growth. Immature people are wise in their own eyes (Romans 1:21-24). They reject truth from both God and people who wish to help.

With God, anyone can become mature. But when immature people harden their hearts to Christ, they suppress the truth of their own wickedness—or so they try (Isaiah 29:15). No matter how much we ignore our evil, it always finds us out (Number 32:23); God leaves no excuse for continued sin (Romans 1:20). That said, he does not force people to accept him, and we must be discerning in the friends we keep (Revelation 3:20; 1 Corinthians 15:33). "People will be lovers of themselves, lovers of money, boastful, proud, abusive, disobedient to their parents, ungrateful, unholy, without love, unforgiving, slanderous, without self-control, brutal, not lovers of the good, treacherous, rash, conceited, lovers of pleasure rather than lovers of God—having a form of godliness but denying its power. Have nothing to do with such people" (2 Timothy 3: 2-5).

Are you drawn to immature people? Are you an immature person? Do you find yourself obsessing over the various diagnoses listed on Google? Stop. Take a break and study only Jesus. He is the epitome of maturity. Any trait or behavior that clashes with his character is sinful. This practice of comparison will help you identify immaturity in both others and yourself.

Day 3

Racial Healing

Galatians 3:26-29

"You speak English well—where are you *really* from?"

"You passed the test because Asians are good at math."

"I bet your son will be a basketball star one day."

As a black Kenyan woman living in the United States, I am all too familiar with statements and questions like these. Such microaggressions target people's affiliation with groups that are often discriminated against or stereotyped. The key reason microaggressions are so disconcerting is that they happen casually, frequently, and often unconsciously.

Even unintended, seemingly-innocent comments can take a toll on the mental health of a marginalized person. Microaggressions breed depression and anger, sometimes impairing performance at school or work. Wounds from racism run especially deep. Racism is a sensitive subject that affects many people groups to some degree. Healing comes with the understanding that the root of racism is sin (John 7:24). Pride makes people look down on others. But we are equal (Romans 2:11).

Some people call COVID-19 the great equalizer—which is partly true. But I'd argue that the greatest equalizer is our sinful human nature and its resulting death (2 Corinthians 5:10). Ethnicity makes no difference; we are all desperate for a Savior. We all need forgiveness. We long to be loved, to feel accepted and to know our worth. God's kingdom is the place where everyone can come together in unity. "Consequently, you are no longer foreigners and aliens, but fellow citizens with God's people and members of God's household, built on the foundation of the apostles and prophets, with Christ Jesus himself as the chief cornerstone. In him the whole building is joined together and rises to become a holy temple in the Lord. And n him you too are being built together to become a dwelling in which God lives by his Spirit" (Ephesians 2:19-22).

When we clothe ourselves in our new identity in Christ, our words and actions change. Microaggressions turn to edifying speech that promotes unity. If I were to conduct a peaceful protest against racism and discrimination today, I would take to the streets and chant the words of Paul: "One Lord, one faith, one baptism; one God and Father of all, who is over all and through all and in all" (Ephesians 4:5-6).

Has racism left festering wounds in your soul? Think about how God forgives your unpardonable offenses. Can you extend the same mercy to others? Have you ever participated in a protest against racism? Consider the chants. Did they promote peace or division? What words from the Bible would be more effective and loving?

Day 4

The Secret

Psalm 139:7-12

When I volunteered at an orphanage in Nairobi, the workers told me horrifying stories about the sexual abuse our children had endured at a previous orphanage. I struggled to understand how God's presence could dwell in places where children are defiled by the very people meant to care for them. If God were there, such abhorrent things could never happen—he would stop them. Right?

In 2013, I became agnostic. I was simply not convinced God exists. If he did, I told myself, he would not allow so much pain and suffering. God heard my doubts. Resurrecting memories buried deep in my mind, he showed me how he was with me in the midst of my own trauma. With fresh eyes, I registered his presence for the first time. He was there when it happened. He was there when my innocence was robbed. Why would he leave me in my darkest hour? There is no doubt in my mind that he saw everything. How else would he know that I needed healing? He was right there. The whole time. And it hurt him just as much as it hurt me.

I too was molested. Although I was only fourteen when it happened, I remember that night as though it were yesterday. If only

I had told my parents what happened in that dark room. If only I had gone to them for help. Instead, I chose to handle the violation on my own. I have always believed myself strong enough to face difficult situations alone. And I didn't know the right words to explain what my cousin had done. Acting like nothing had happened, I kept my secret for nearly three decades. But the memory haunted me. A few years after the incident, my cousin took his own life. There was no way I could tell anyone about his crime now. I didn't want to cause his family more pain. But bottling up the abuse spawned a root of bitterness and anger that would fester over time into depression and anxiety. Crippled by my untended wound, I looked to ungodly men for completion. My symptoms worsened as I jumped from bad relationship to bad relationship until, finally, I hit rock bottom in 2018. It was then that I left my last unhealthy relationship and began my journey toward healing.

Twenty-six years later, I was ready to speak out. I called my dad and unveiled the childhood trauma that had propelled me into a cycle of dysfunctional relationships with men. After praying over me, he told me he was glad I opened up to him. As a child, I lacked the courage to admit that such a shameful thing happened to me. But hiding the truth altered our relationship. I didn't feel like daddy's little girl anymore. Instead, I felt polluted and ugly. All I have wanted since that wretched day is to be daddy's little girl again. It took me a long time to realize that the only thing needed to restore the strong bond we once shared was honesty.

For what felt like a lifetime, I harbored a poisonous secret because I was afraid my dad would reject me if he knew the truth. How wrong I was. He showed me nothing but the deepest love and under-standing. My only regret is that I didn't tell him sooner. Who knows what better route my life might have taken. I could have avoided so much of the heartache and pain that accompanied my toxic adult relationships. My dad may not have known my secret, but God knew. There is nowhere we can hide from his presence (Psalm 139:7-12). He sees all things (Proverbs 15:3).

God was there all along. He never left my side. Even in my darkest, most shameful hour, he watched over me and led me back home. He proved his love when he died on the cross to pay for my sins—centuries before I was born and had the chance to repent (Romans 5:8). God did not condone my cousin's abusing me (Psalm 5:4). But I can now see why he allowed it. Through my suffering, he taught me forgiveness. Had the offense never occurred, I would not know today what it means to forgive someone of an act so evil. Further, as a healed survivor of sexual assault, I can help others face their journeys of healing from abuse (Romans 8:28).

God is waiting for you to turn toward him (2 Peter 3:9). Once you do, he will run to you (Luke 15:20). He will shatter walls, climb mountains, leap rivers, and swim oceans to reach you. "Everyone who calls on the name of the Lord will be saved" (Roman's 10:13). Though he won't force you to accept him, there is absolutely nothing you can do to stop him from loving you (Joshua 24:15; Romans 8:39).

I feel so free now that my secret no longer holds power over me. The longer I cowered in darkness, the more Satan used the darkness against me. Now that the evil I experienced is exposed by the light, healing is inevitable (Ephesians 5:13). Instead of catering to the desires of my flesh, I can make choices that honor and glorify God (Galatians 5:16).

What secrets are you harboring? How have shame and guilt affected you? Your relationships? Is there someone you can open up to? Pray for the courage to bring your wounds into the light and let God heal them.

Day 5

Eagle in the Chicken Coop

Psalm 103:2-5

In the spring of 2019, I arrived at the Shunem Christian Retreat Centre in Embu, Kenya. I stayed there for one week with Ellel Ministries International—a non-profit, healing organization that impacted my life. Through Ellel, God restored my wings so I could soar like an eagle—high in the sky and close to him, where I belong.

While I was at the retreat, God gave me a vision of an eagle trapped in a chicken coop. The eagle's feathers had been plucked off by the chickens, and a rooster was violently pecking her to the point of helplessness. She had no wings to carry her to safety. The image raised many questions: What was an eagle doing in a chicken coop? Who put her there? How did a bird of prey find herself trapped among chickens?

God gave me clarity in that moment. There is an eagle in the chicken coop. I am that eagle. Once upon a time, I flew high above the trees, soaring with the wind. I was untouchable— strong, independent, and free to serve God. Gliding on wings of faith, I met with him regularly, praying and listening for his voice. I enjoyed our quiet time together and was not easily influenced by the cares or vanities of this world. Then one day, I spotted a silver cage glinting beneath some branches. It looked comfortable, with plush straw to nest in and fresh grains to eat. The wired walls guaranteed safety from wild animals and rest for tired wings. The chickens inside clucked disapprovingly at my flapping wings. "Join us," they said. "Life in a cage is much easier." And so, I descended from God's side, trading purpose for pleasure as I locked myself in. As a rush of sharp beaks greeted me, I realized too late that I had been tricked, trapped by my own passions and worldly desires.

Chickens live in flocks, pecking each other to assert dominance and gaining submission through fear and pain—much like how the world operates without Christ. For some reason, I was convinced I could survive in the chicken coop. Surely a great eagle like myself could handle a few little chickens. Maybe I could change them, teach them to glide like eagles. But chickens don't fly, and eagles don't flock. How can such different birds coexist?

The moment my wings brushed the straw, the chickens were on me, plucking my feathers one by one: self-worth, identity, ambition, independence, solitude with God. The cage that had promised me refuge stripped everything away. I couldn't hear God's voice over the fracas of squawking beaks and scratching talons. But one day, when my tattered soul could fight no longer, I cried out to him and he heard me. Throwing my cage door open, he ushered me free from the raging chickens, bandaged my wings, and restored my soul. With each broken piece he stitched back together, I rose a little higher. And before I could comprehend the love that had rescued me, I was soaring—God at my side once more. I will never return to that chicken coop. I am an eagle. My home is the sky.

You, too, are an eagle. Has the devil clipped your wings, trapped you in a rusty cage with no key? Jesus wants to save your soul and heal your wounds: "Come to me all you who are weary and burdened and I will give you rest" (Matthew 11:28). As with newly-hatched chicks, your first steps in the light will be difficult. Slowly, your eyes will adjust to God's radiance. And before you know it, his rays will shimmer on your beating wings. Once you've embraced the new life God has prepared, you will never be the same. Find your freedom. Say yes to Jesus today.

What temptations call to you from inside the chicken coop? How have you given into them? Are the people in your life pushing you to greater heights, or are unhealthy relationships tearing out your feathers? What choices can you make to ensure your return to the skies?

To Know Thy God
Is to Know Thyself

Philippians 3:7-11

K now the makeup of your body, soul, and mind—and recognize its worth. This step is the beginning of your journey toward the deepest love any human being could experience. To know God is to know yourself. You are made in the image and likeness of God (Genesis 1:27).

God gave you authority to rule the resources (not people) he provides. For example, I discovered and harnessed my aptitude for creative writing and self-discipline. No one is governing me, or forcing me to pursue my goals. I am compelled by my love for God and by his promise to bless the works of my hands (Deuteronomy 28:12).

God has granted each of us the ability to be disciplined and obedient to his call in our lives. He has put a special gift inside you. If you spend quality time with God, digging deep into his Word and meditating on his truth, you will unwrap that gift. He will unveil passions and talents you never knew you had. Don't be like the servant who buried his talent (Matthew 25:25). Take what you have and multiply it for the good of others and the glory of God.

God is doing a good work in you behind the scenes. God tinkers on our hearts without us even knowing. In his time, he will elevate you to a position in which your gift can bless others and point them to Jesus (Ecclesiastes 3:11).

Do you struggle to spend time alone with God? If so, why? List your distractions and brainstorm solutions to help you carve out more alone time with God.

Day 7
Mapping Your Spiritual Journey
Psalm 51:1-12

Age of Innocence. The age of innocence is characterized by excitement, playfulness, creativity, and a sense of completeness, a time of freedom and grandiose dreams. Most of us can recall a phase in our childhoods when nothing was impossible to achieve. We expected to be astronauts, brain surgeons, Olympians, war generals, master chefs, superheroes, president, lion tamers or even royalty. There was nothing in our innocent young minds to inhibit imagination. It is during the age of innocence that we are most open to receiving Jesus in our hearts—and are most susceptible to falling for false doctrines that will warp the foundation of our identity. As children, we were full of trusting expectancy; the world was warm and bright. Life was sweet—until one day, something woke us up and shattered the illusion.

Death of Innocence. Abuse, neglect, divorce, loss of a loved one, and sickness are just a few childhood experiences that can cause lifelong trauma. This period is characterized by pain, sadness, confusion, disappointment, despair, and a feeling of betrayal. Things happened that you were too young to understand, events with consequences even adults struggle to comprehend. Often, affected children see their trauma resurface during adulthood. Residual pain grows a bitter root in one's soul, with each day lengthening the healing process. We tend to bury unpleasant experiences deep in our subconscious—but hidden wounds never really go away. They will manifest in new ways down the road.

Descent. The next stage of the spiritual journey is likely a time of questioning everything. Childhood trauma comes out in fornication, alcoholism, substance abuse, parent disobedience, violence, and other acts of rebellion. The young heart feels immortal, free to pursue whatever it desires. Thus, begins a slow decline as we turn away from God. Eventually, we become so jaded and enmeshed in sin that we can no longer hear the Holy Spirit convicting us. Our hearts grow cold, calloused to the things of God.

Rock Bottom. There comes a point at which we realize that the lust of the flesh cannot be quenched. Nothing in this world satisfies. We have failed in our attempt to numb the pain of childhood trauma and are forced to accept that the only way to break free of our baggage is to face it. This period is characterized by anxiety, fear, depression, hopelessness, and shame. At rock bottom, we feel the depths of worthlessness, afraid we have lost our identity forever. It is in this valley that we cry out for God to rescue us.

The Journey Back. God always catches us when we fall. Guiding us back to himself in loving and supernatural ways, he helps us accept what we cannot understand, forgive those we considered unforgiveable, own up to our faults, and take steps toward a restored future. He asks us to repent for the bitterness we've harbored in our hearts, offering unlimited mercy, grace, and salvation. This is the redemption he promises.

Return to Innocence. "I tell you the truth, anyone who doesn't receive the kingdom of God like a child will never enter it" (Mark 10:15). The Holy Spirit is the Wonderful Counselor who leads us back to innocence. Now an adult under God's wing, you can better understand that the evil events marring your childhood were attacks of the enemy beyond your control. It is time to start your journey toward forgiveness. Forgiveness is a process able to place only once we realize the immeasurable forgiveness God has shown us. True forgiveness is marked by the belief that there is power in the death and resurrection of Christ to cover the sins of those who sin against us. Jesus said "forgive them father, for they know not what they do" (Luke 23:34). We do not excuse the evil, we call it out for what it is. Forgiveness is releasing them from our punishment because vengeance belongs to the Lord (Romans 12:19).

The Holy Spirit will reveal what God really thinks about you. He will reveal the lies you have believed all these years and guide you to truth. I have walked this journey; it is an uphill battle. It is not easy. Very few people are willing to go to those dark places, but walking the valley with God is necessary if you want to heal. It is so worth it. I went through each stage of the spiritual journey described and I am a testimony of God's promise: you can return back to the place of joy, love, hope, and peace. You will dream again. You will create again. The child who was buried deep inside will come out to play. You will be stronger and wiser, knowing exactly who you are and whose you are: a child of God, bought with the precious blood of Jesus.

If you want to live the abundant life God offers, you must seek his righteousness. "Seek first the kingdom of God and his righteousness and all these things shall be given to you as well" (Matthew 6:33).

Write about your spiritual journey, from the joyful days of innocent to the place you are right now. Do you notice any patterns? Write down the names of people you need to forgive. Write down the names of people you hurt and desire forgiveness from. Healing comes when we speak the truth. I pray that you find the courage to confess your sins. God is merciful to forgive and heal you.

Day 8

The Summit of Identity Healing

2 Corinthians 5:17

T he healing journey is an uphill battle. There are several mountains to climb. The first summit God had me scale was that of finding my identity in Christ. Though fierce storms tried to batter me and jagged stones tripped me, I kept climbing. Sometimes I feared I might faint from exhaustion. The worldly way would be so much easier. After all, the world's path is smooth, straight, and downhill—the ultimate temptation for a weary soul. But just when I was about to call it quits, I saw bright flags whipping above the peak. I had made it to the top. Now able to see my rocky path from beginning to the end, I can share the truths God taught me along the way. There was a reason and a purpose for everything. God was working even when I could not see him.

The view from the mountaintop is beautiful, calm, and less crowded than the trail. God's voice rings clearer. The air is fresh, my joy overflows, and my heart is full of peace. Waves of relief wash over me. My soul has been restored and my heart renewed. I am patient with myself and others. I am less judgmental of others and I leave room for their faults (Colossians 3:13). My words are kinder, seasoned with God's truth and compassion. My breath is deeper, my love more sacrificial, and my body healthier. The pain from my past is faded and more bearable. My awareness of how much I need God is greater.

But the work is not done yet, there are other layers of character to build. God doesn't want us to loiter alone in this journey. He tells us to keep going, to help others struggling to conquer the same trail. Discipleship is about humility. It is God who works in us to will and to act according to his good purpose (Philippians 2:13). The fruit of the Christlike spirit is a life focused on encouraging others to continue the race without losing heart.

Are you at the top of a mountain? Have you gotten comfortable up there? Stay too long, and you'll find yourself plagued with spiritual altitude sickness: a nasty combination of pride and judgement of others. Don't risk stumbling off the edge. Come down and help others along their journey. You will discover new flaws in yourself and new perfections in God. Though it can be scary, I love allowing God to show me my weaknesses so we can mend them one at a time together. I pray daily that God continues to refine me. Lord, please mould and shape me to look more like you.

What trials or problems are you working through? Do you feel swallowed in a dark valley, that even the mountain's base is out of reach? Tell God. How do you imagine the mountaintop will look once you have braved the journey? What steps can you take to better trust God as he guides you up steep cliffs to the sunny peak? If you're already flying high, think about ways you can help others climb to meet you.

PART II
Knowing God

Day 9

Where Are You, God?

Psalm 10:1-18

A re you in the midst of a crisis? Feeling utterly alone, abandoned by a God who's out of reach? Are you lost with no way out? I have spent many hours in God's presence, pleading with him to alleviate my pain. There were times I sat in my suffering for days before finally seeing a breakthrough. Although the Lord does occasionally give clear, instant answers, more often than not he requires a process of seeking. Why? Because the act of drawing near to God is an important part of relationship that takes time—sometimes a lot of time—and is not always easy. I have discovered great beauty in the act of waiting. The treasure God reveals at the end is well worth the hard work and faith.

Be patient with yourself in this process. It has taken me 25 years to finally reach a place at which I am not struggling to hear God. I have spent hours with therapists and flipped through dozens of self-help books. I've dedicated countless mornings to writing in my journal, asking questions and seeking God. Eventually I grew weary, giving up on my quest and approaching life as if God were just a figment of my imagination. That was the biggest mistake I ever made. Exhausted and lonely, I stopped searching.

In 2013, after the death of my best friend, I moved home to Kenya and resumed life like God did not exist. I didn't pray or read my Bible intentionally, attending church every Sunday purely out of habit. After a while, the outside noise of the world drowned out God's still small voice. This was my descent. I was lost. Things went from bad to worse when I got married. I sank deeper into the abyss of misplaced identity. I was desperate, lonely, adrift, and in need of a Savior. I didn't find God. He found me and pulled me out of the darkness.

It is in our brokenness that we turn to God. When we are vulnerable, we become willing to listen. When we slow down and quiet our minds, muting the cries of the world, we begin to hear God's still small voice (1 Kings 19:11-13). He is speaking.

How have recent events in your life led you to want to hear from God? In what ways, both small and big, does God remind you of his presence? Pause. Listen. Can you hear him? Read his Word. What is he saying?

Day 10

Is God Good?

Psalm 145:3-9

Have you ever doubted God's goodness after being hurt by people you believe to be Christians? Have you been deeply injured by people you looked up to, people who claimed to be God-fearing followers of Jesus while shamelessly watching you suffer? Has your pain led you to wonder if God is truly good? If there is even a hint of doubt in your mind, the devil will exploit it to feed you lies about God's character. The truth, proven through both his actions and Word, is that God *is* good (Psalm 100:5). It is only when we allow the devil to infiltrate our minds that we doubt God's goodness. Satan uses clever manipulation and half-truths to keep bind us in our own beliefs.

In 2013, while living in Guam, I questioned God's goodness after the death of my best friend and mentor, Mia Tomada. I was angry at God because he didn't allow us the chance to fulfill our dream of working as full-time missionaries in the Pacific Islands. Mia desired to live among unreached people groups and preach the gospel. I felt betrayed when she died. After all, I had stood with her in faith, believing that God would heal her lung cancer and render her strong and healthy, able to fulfill her dreams. But that didn't happen. My anger seeped like a bitter root into every area of my life.

Upon Mia's death, I left Guam and moved back home to Kenya. In my fragile state, I volunteered at a government-operated children's home in Nairobi. The experience that followed made me question the very existence of God. I witnessed an obscene violation of human rights at a facility. I learned from an inside source that the children were being neglected and abused, with living conditions worse than those of a prison. I asked the director of the home if he was aware of the atrocities and if he could produce a sustainable plan of action. I didn't get the response I hoped for. There was no plan for the children's future except to be minimally fed, clothed, and housed.

Why was the church doing nothing to end the suffering of these children? I was confused. Nairobi is the fastest growing metropolis in Africa, a home to megachurches worth millions of shillings—yet the most vulnerable population was being neglected. My heart hardened as a bitter root against the church took hold. I wanted nothing to do with Christianity if it was going to make me like those church leaders more concerned about personal success than about the wellbeing of vulnerable children.

I took my dreams to serve God and buried them in the ground. My soul was sick. The corruption of leadership in both the church and the government had crumbled my faith. I felt too insignificant to do anything about the injustice I saw. So I pointed fingers at God, sank my dreams, and went about my life. I married someone who knew about God but never professed his belief publicly. I knew he lied about his job and how much money he made. I ignored all the red flags, making excuses for the things he did that bothered me. We were both stranded in the same boat of trying to figure out life, driven by a desperate need to be rescued. The problem was that we were looking to each other for salvation.

It was then that I dove into the darkest season of my life. For three years, I acted like I didn't need God. My husband became my idol, my everything. Life was miserable. I could write a book on how to ensure the unhappiest marriage possible. Although my marriage contributed to my emptiness, the truth is that it wasn't the actual source—a realization that came only recently. I was unhappy and unfulfilled before ever saying "I do." Marriage just brought out the worst in me. It exposed all the pain and brokenness I had buried inside. You cannot produce fruit when your heart is encased in bitterness, resentment, and pain from the past. You must deal with your emotional and spiritual junk before entering a marriage. I learned the hard way. Having faced my internal tangles after the fact —better late than never—I feel ready for God to entrust me with more responsibility.

God allows us to suffer trials because ultimately, they alert us to our need for him, and that is when we submit to his will, we see his goodness tangibly. (And although his goodness does not always ensure our happiness, it always ensures our joy and holiness.) The goodness of God is reflected in how he disciplines us like a loving father so we can be more like him.

Write about a time you doubted God's goodness. Was your skepticism caused by a significant loss, failure, or injury? You are not alone. Write an angry letter and pour out your heart to God. He is near to the brokenhearted (Psalm 34:18). Your season of healing has just begun.

Day 11

God Works Behind the Scenes

Psalm 23:1-6

I t is the year 2020, and millions of people across the globe have
been forced into quarantine by the COVID-19 pandemic. The
world has never seen anything like this in all of history.

People are treading water, trying desperately to stay afloat in a
season of uncertainty, fear, and worry. Some of us have lost jobs or
even loved ones to the virus. We are struggling financially, spiritually,
mentally, and socially, forced to isolate ourselves in our homes and
disconnect from the rest of society. Do you feel cut off from the rest
of the world, unsure when things will get better? Your inner battle is
real. These are perilous times. But in the midst of it all, God is near.

This season of darkness you've found yourself stumbling through
might be leading you to question your identity—perhaps even your
existence. Maybe your relationships have taken a hit. I've seen
COVID-19 dash marriages against the rocks and spike the rates of
depression and suicide. People are searching for hope. Jesus under-
stands our suffering because he went through it too. He was betrayed
by his best friends and felt forsaken by his own Father: "Jesus cried

out in a loud voice…'My God, my God, why have you forsaken me?'" (Matthew 27:46)

Even in chaos and confusion, God is sovereign. Sometimes he uses adversity to refine the areas of our spirits that need growth. Take a peek backstage, the place where God does some of his most transformational work. Although it is tempting, don't pray for God to rid you of trials—instead ask him for the strength to endure. Believe that he is leading you through the valley, shaping your character and deepening your faith as you walk together. He will give you the perseverance to handle the work set before you.

God is preparing you for greater responsibility. To receive it, you must stay near the cross and on your knees. Jesus is calling, urging you to give your life to him in surrender. Ask him to heal your heart and show you the way into his kingdom. The Holy Spirit will guide you to the truth. Open your Bible and read Isaiah 61. Jesus came to set the captives free.

Have you ever experienced a season of isolation? What lessons did you learn? If you recently lost a job, relationship, or hobby, how can you maximize the extra time you have been given?

Day 12

Jesus Came to Set Us Free

Isaiah 61:1-11

There is freedom for slaves and captives! The universal key to all of humanity's chains is the gospel. Jesus has the power to free you from oppression. Your enemy, the devil, wields oppression like a sword, be it systemic injustice, modern-day slavery, addiction, depression, or other bondage. I think long and hard about my mission statement before I go into the mission field. I want it to reflect exactly what Jesus taught, staying true to Christ's mission for us to preach his gospel (Matthew 28:19). He came to set the captives free, and so should we (Luke 4:18). Isaiah 61:1-3 proclaims Jesus' purpose in the world, illustrating his mission to bring freedom from sin:

The Spirit of the Sovereign Lord is on me,
>   because the Lord has anointed me
>   to proclaim good news to the poor.
He has sent me to bind up the brokenhearted,
>   to proclaim freedom for the captives
>   and release from darkness for the prisoners,
>   to proclaim the year of the Lord's favor
>   and the day of vengeance of our God,
>   to comfort all who mourn,

and provide for those who grieve in Zion—
    to bestow on them a crown of beauty
    instead of ashes,
    the oil of joy
    instead of mourning,
    and a garment of praise
    instead of a spirit of despair.
They will be called oaks of righteousness,
    a planting of the Lord
    for the display of his splendor.

Jesus loves broken people by mending and healing them. Some people enjoy fixing broken gadgets like cars and electronics. I enjoy coming alongside people with broken hearts and damaged souls so I can witness the miracle of Jesus' healing as we walk together. I love seeing how a person can transform into a whole new being (2 Corinthians 5:17). It's so beautiful! I am a passionate advocate for those who cannot speak for themselves. I want to give a voice to the voiceless and fight for the rights of people unaware of their value. "Speak up for those who cannot speak for themselves, for the rights of all who are destitute. Speak up and judge fairly. Defend the rights of the poor and needy" (Proverbs 31:8-9).

Anything I do for people the world deems insignificant and unworthy, I do as an honor to God (Matthew 25:40). His image is imprinted into every human being. "Whoever oppresses the poor shows contempt for their Maker, but whoever is kind to the needy honors God" (Proverbs 14:31).

Are you wary of participating in social causes because you fear being labeled "liberal," "progressive," or "secular"? What does the Bible say about the importance of combatting issues that plague the poor and voiceless? How can you overcome your fear of man and take up arms for Jesus (Proverbs 29:25; 2 Timothy 1:7)?

Day 13

God Meets Us Where We Are

Matthew 18:12

It is impossible to escape from God. He pursues us relentlessly. We cannot run from his presence or hope to win a game of hide-and-seek (Psalm 139:1-12). God is omnipresent and omniscient, everywhere at all times and aware of all things. His love follows us to the greatest heights, the darkest depths, and the farthest corners. He will never abandon us. "Can a mother forget the baby at her breast and have no compassion on the child she has borne? Though she may forget, I will not forget you!

See, I have engraved you on the palms of my hands; your walls are ever before me" (Isaiah 49:15-16).

Have you ever tried playing hide-and-seek with a toddler? It's hilarious! When you tell the child to hide, she stands in the middle of the room, closes her eyes, and puts her little hands over her face. Toddlers truly believe that if they can't see you, then you can't see them. Sometimes we try disappearing the same way. But how can we hide from a God who is omnipresent and omniscient? We cower behind our guilt and shame, clinging to masks and the lie that God cannot see through to our pain, sin, or brokenness. Our minds deceive us into believing that God is absent. But he stands by, still and quiet, watching us—a loving father playing hide-and-seek with his little child. "I still see you!" he says with a smile. He knows we are weak and misguided, so he waits patiently, drawing us tenderly to himself as we open our eyes.

In a way, the disgruntled Christian's threat to "never return to church again" is amusing. Why? Because God is everywhere—not just in a church building. If you choose to flee from Sunday-morning church services, don't be surprised when you encounter an influx of messages reminding you of his presence, that he still sees you and is able to speak through anything or anyone. You simply cannot escape the love of God. He is the Good Shepherd who leaves the flock in search of his one lost sheep (Matthew 18:12). The church doors may close, perhaps because of a pandemic or war, but the gospel makes its way through people, events, stories, actions, art, dreams, and social media. God will find you—even in the deepest, darkest places.

In what unexpected places has God found you? How did he get your attention? Saturate yourself in the knowledge that your heavenly Father will never, ever leave you. There is no use trying to hide from his love.

Day 14

He Restores My Soul

Psalm 91:5-16

When restoring broken hearts, God is kind, eager to forgive and cleanse us of sin. He handles us with patience, the gentlest touch. Yet our human tendency is to rush the healing process. If we jump up prematurely, ignoring God's caution that he has not yet finished tending to our wounds, we risk crumbling back to the ground.

Allow the Lord time to heal your spirit and establish your identity. He will restore your full armor, giving you strength through the power of the Holy Spirit. He will speak to you daily as you spend quality time with him. If you recently experienced the breakup of a relationship, wait for God to put the pieces of your heart back together before you start dating again. (I'm speaking from personal experience).

People who disregard God's timing operate from old identities and typically end up choosing someone detrimental to their emotional and spiritual health. Rebounds might offer temporary pleasure and relief from pain, but they ultimately lead straight back to the old patterns that broke you in the first place. Don't cave to insecurity or grief. Instead, let God use your experience to grow you, to reinforce your foundation so you stand firm on Christ, the solid rock (Matthew 7:25). Humble yourself and know that it's God who gives you strength and fights for you. Without his full armor and aid, we cannot win our battles (Ephesians 6:11-17). Trust in the promises that comforted David (Psalm 91:1-6, 14-16):

Whoever dwells in the shelter of the Most High
    will rest in the shadow of the Almighty.
I will say of the Lord, "He is my refuge and my fortress,
    my God, in whom I trust."
Surely he will save you
    from the fowler's snare
    and from the deadly pestilence.
He will cover you with his feathers,
    and under his wings you will find refuge;
    his faithfulness will be your shield and rampart.
You will not fear the terror of night,
    nor the arrow that flies by day,
    nor the pestilence that stalks in the darkness,
    nor the plague that destroys at midday.

"Because he loves me," says the Lord, "I will rescue him;
    I will protect him, for he acknowledges my name.
He will call on me, and I will answer him;
    I will be with him in trouble,
    I will deliver him and honor him.

With long life I will satisfy him
and show him my salvation."

Tell God about your broken heart and ask him to glue the pieces back together. He loves you so deeply. Let him heal your soul.

Day 15

Transformation in the Wilderness

Psalm 63:1-11

C onsider Joseph, David, Daniel, and other figures in the Bible who stood up for righteousness and were abused. Despite their loyalty to God, they ended up as outcasts, prisoners, and even lunchmeat for lions. Although innocent, they were tortured, maligned, and rejected. Why did God allow such mistreatment? Because it is in solitude and suffering that he transforms lives and reveals his glory. Like God's people in the Bible, we too come out of the wilderness with new wisdom, character, humility, and faith.

Through Joseph's enslavement and captivity (Genesis 37, 39-40), God transformed him into a man of integrity and strength, able to bless people with the wealth, status, and power God would bestow upon him (Genesis 41-47). During his years of suffering, Joseph allowed God to replace his bitterness and rage with humble surrender. Instead of destroying the brothers who ripped him from his father and sold him into Egyptian slavery, Joseph forgave them—an act that required immense grace. Imagine the pain he might have inflicted on his brothers had God not transformed him (Genesis 45:1-28). God is a merciful Father, never allowing the sinfulness of individuals to destroy his chosen people. During the seven-year famine that followed his instatement as vizier, Joseph saved both Israel and Egypt from starvation. God took what a few sinful people meant for evil and used it for the good of nations (Genesis 50:20).

Perhaps a loved one has betrayed you, poisoning your heart with bitterness and spite. Pause. Allow God time to heal you. Ask him for the grace to handle your situation with compassion and kindness. Suffering is the crucible in which God purifies our thoughts and intentions. It is possible to honor God even during divorce, finalizing the separation with dignity because you belong to Christ. I used my time of separation to revamp my self-worth, resisting the temptation to date around and fulfill my fleshly desires. It was hard, but God gave me strength. We are called to be salt and light to the world (Matthew 5:13-14). Let your light shine even in court while you navigate legal battles. Pray, read the Bible, and listen to God as he guides you through turmoil. Trust that he is remaking your heart, replacing hatred with love and discord with peace.

God has guided me through the wildernesses of loss, betrayal, and separation. Although it is natural and tempting to react to pain, I learned to hesitate and consider the consequences of my actions. For example, I had to resist the temptation to label my ex-husband with the narcissistic personality disorder because he has not been diagnosed. I see a trend on social media where people are just throwing the term loosely without evidence that their spouses have the condition. The problem with focusing too much on the abuser, is that it leads to the victim mentality and blaming everything on them.

You must be patient during your healing journey. Resist the urge to harm yourself with gluttony, alcohol, gossip, or slander. Surround yourself with people who are truthful and life-giving. Find healthy outlets for your pain: art, fellowship, exercise, service, nature, prayer, and so on. When we dwell on revenge and allow hurt to fester, it is impossible to sit and enjoy the sunset, to smile in the refreshing breeze of a hot summer day. Guilt is a perpetual tormenter. When we trust that there is purpose in our suffering, that God is using the wilderness to bring us closer to him—it is then that we experience the transformation that brings forgiveness. The wisdom, kindness, and joy rewarded by faithful perseverance through pain usher us directly into God's presence and love.

Describe your wilderness. How is God using suffering to transform you? How has he done so in the past? What can you be grateful for as you endure the crucible of love?

Day 16

The Ultimate Sacrifice

Isaiah 52:1-12

B ecause God's children are human beings made of flesh and blood, Jesus also became flesh and blood (John 1:14). For only as a human could he die, accepting pain and suffering beyond what we will ever experience—just to preserve a relationship with us while glorifying God (Isaiah 53:5). It was his death and resurrection alone that broke the power of the evil one to destroy us. Only the cross can set us free from death (Acts 4:12).

We also know that the Son did not come to save angels but to save the descendants of Adam. Therefore, it was necessary for him to become like us in *every* way (Philippians 2:7). This is why he took on the role of merciful High Priest before God (Hebrews 4:14-15). He offered the ultimate sacrifice to absolve mankind (John 3:16). Because he voluntarily welcomed human tribulation and testing, he is able to personally help us in our own trials.

I can't fathom sacrificing my dreams, my comfort, my career—certainly not my life—to pay off someone else's credit card debt. But Jesus did not hesitate to offer himself, a perfectly righteous and holy being, to redeem the very sinners who condemned him to death (2

Corinthians 5:21). He did not owe any debt, yet he paid the ultimate sacrifice so that everyone who believes in him can be set free from sin. All we must do to be saved is confess Christ as Lord, turn from our wicked ways, and walk in the light of his love (Romans 10:9).

There is so much freedom in a life with Christ. In Ephesians 2:10, Paul tells us to walk in the works God planned for us before the beginning of time. Once we internalize the sacrifice Christ made to ensure our salvation, once we stop striving to prove ourselves—only then we can find rest and enjoy what the Lord has in store (1 John 1:9).

What's the greatest sacrifice you've ever made? Who was it for? How did it feel to give up so much? Imagine making the same sacrifice for someone you cannot stand, for someone who would likely never appreciate it. Tough, right? Jesus did infinitely more when he died on the cross. Take a moment to reflect on what he did for you.

Day 17

His Love Is Amazing

Romans 5:6-11

G od's love is unfathomable. It seems unbelievable to us because
we don't love like he does. Unlike humans, the heavenly Father
loves us not because of who we are but because of who he is. He
loves us the same way he loves Jesus. He is the essence of love. His
love is without motive. We don't deserve his love, but he cherishes us
beyond measure. God's love has no breaking point. And nothing
forms a tender heart like the realization that one is so deeply and
sincerely loved.

One of the primary reasons God encourages prayer is that he
wants us to spend time basking in his love. His love is so overwhelming
that, to those who are perishing, it seems foolish and unrelatable (1
Corinthians 1:18). Some religious leaders package what appears to be
a more tangible definition of love, catering to the demands of a
perplexed congregation. Humans can relate to works-based religion.
After all, we are full of pride and the desire to govern ourselves. It
takes immense humility to accept sacrificial love.

Jesus, who chose to descend to Earth as a human, remained fully
God and demonstrated God's love (John 10:30). He healed lepers

and associated with prostitutes and tax collectors. This kind of love was novel to humanity, impossible to understand. Jesus emphasized relationship, but for many, religion seemed more attainable, doable, practical, comfortable, perhaps easy. It certainly required less humility and most people choose this road (Matthew 7:13-14).

How did Jesus do it? How could he sacrifice so much, pouring time, energy, and ultimately blood into the salvation of lowly humans who didn't even want him? I believe the key is the tremendous amount of time Jesus spent in God's presence. He knew the Father, and the Father knew him. I too want to know God so well that my love for others imitates his: unconditional, deep, and unrestrained.

In what ways has God demonstrated his love for you? List some, from big to small. You might be surprised by the thought God puts into details. Spend more time soaking up God's love so you can pour it into others.

Day 18

The Wonderful Counselor

Isaiah 9:1-21

I have the best therapist and helper: the Holy Spirit. He gave me the strength to tackle this project. Jesus is the Wonderful Counselor. He heals my diseases, the wounds in my soul. Fellowshipping with God every morning is better than the best counseling session! He is available whenever I need him, for as long as I want. And it's free—much more cost effective than a human therapist!

Jesus is a gentleman; he knocks on the door of your heart and waits for you to open it (Revelation 3:20). Once you invite him in, he will heal you, showing you hope and the promise of a good future. Connect with him, and he will give you access to the entire kingdom. Don't be like the prodigal son's older brother (Luke 15:11-32). The father wanted an intimate relationship with both children, but the older son was not interested in joining his father's feast: "The older brother became angry and refused to go in. So his father went out and pleaded with him. But he answered his father, 'Look! All these years I've been slaving for you and never disobeyed your orders. Yet you never gave me even a young goat so I could celebrate with my friends. But when this son of yours who has squandered your property with prostitutes comes home, you kill the fattened calf for him!" (Luke 15:28-30)

Jesus wants to feast with you, to have an intimate relationship with you. He wants to save you from your pride, the lust of the eyes, and the lust of the flesh. He wants to protect you from the human nature that leads you down the path of self-destruction. Trust him. He is the way, the truth, and the life (John 14:6).

Imagine you are sitting in your first session with the best therapist in the world. What help do ask for? Now take that request to God. He is the best therapist in the universe.

Day 19

His Ways Are Higher

Matthew 6:33

My mind is too small to comprehend all of God's ways. That's why I will spend eternity in wonder and in awe of him, striving to know him better daily. I haven't even begun to scratch the surface of who God is. His ways are higher than my ways. His thoughts are higher than my thoughts (Isaiah 55:9). He is vaster than the universe, and I am a billion light-years away. In the same way that I cannot see the farthest star in the heavens, I will never be able to fully understand God's ways. Who am I to demand that he explain himself? He reveals exactly what we need to know in the timing he deems fit. Although we understand so little, he has proved to us countless times that he is worthy of our trust.

When on my knees seeking answers, I prepare myself for anything. I prepare myself to forgive others for past, present and future sins. So, I wake up early in the morning to start my day in God's presence so he can expand my capacity to handle the many hurtful things that come my way. His grace is sufficient. He adds to my faith more grace to forgive.

So how will you heal from broken relationships, abuse and pain caused by others? By getting down on our knees in humility and asking God to have mercy on us, to reveal to us our sins and show us how far we have walked away from him. He is requiring that we sacrifice the things that are distracting us from spending time with him in prayer.

There is so much that God has in store for us, but he says, "seek ye first the kingdom of God and his righteousness and all these things will be added unto you" (Matthew 6:33). Our relationship with God is more important than seeking the approval of men. It is more important for us to find our calling and purpose as disciples than to roam around aimlessly trying to find happiness and fulfilment in temporary things.

Where do you go to find answers to life's difficult questions? Are you grappling with concepts too big to wrap your mind around? Read the Bible prayerfully every day, and your eyes will be opened to the truth.

Day 20

A Letter from My Heavenly Father

Psalm 139:1-18

My dearest child,

I am writing you this letter because you are struggling with rejection. I want to heal you and ease your pain. Reflect on my love, a love that existed before you were formed in your mother's womb. I shaped you and know the number of hairs on your head.

No cell of your body goes unnoticed to me. I made you in my image, and you are mine. Even when you walked away from me, I waited for you. I longed for the day you would turn your face toward me. When you did, I ran to you and embraced you as my own. I wiped away your tears. I love you so much. The way you smile, the way you walk. I love your voice and the way you sing for me. I want to open doors for you to express talents I gave you to bless others. Don't allow rejection to isolate you.

Let go and sing. Every morning, I will give you a new song. Just open your mouth, and the words will flow from your soul. I put the love of Jesus in your heart so you would light up the world with love, joy, peace, patience, kindness, goodness, faithfulness, and self-control. You can overcome the world because Jesus overcame the world. I will give you the strength to endure the hardship of rejection. I will carry you when you are wounded.

Don't be afraid to serve others. I will walk with you and guide you. I will warn you against people with evil intentions. I will shield you from those working with the enemy to destroy you. Just walk the path I've set before you and lean on me. I will lead you and guide you. I will cover you in my shelter. I will protect you. Abide in me, and I will abide in you. You will not be snatched by Satan. You are safe. Stay close to me, and I will stay close to you.

With love,
Your heavenly Father

Read Psalm 23, 91, and 139. Meditate on what God's Word says about you, using Scripture to write your own letter from God to you. Then, if you feel so inspired, write him a response.

PART III
Knowing Your Enemy

Day 21

How to Tame a Christian

2 Corinthians 11:13-15

D id you ever visit the circus as a kid? Do you remember watching in awe as a man sporting a striped suit stuck his head inside the mouth of a lion without so much as a flinch? How could such large fangs and sharp claws not strike terror in his heart? From where did the lion tamer get his power over the beast? In a way, the devil resembles a lion tamer. While God has created us to be fierce, emboldening us with his own Spirit, the devil intimidates us into submission. Posturing and prodding, rewarding and punishing, he conditions us into believing we are helpless. Once trained, we cower behind bars at the flick of a whip—a tragic display of the devil's conquest. Proud and full of bravado, the devil is unfazed by weak Christians. He does not fear complacency. But he is terrified of unbroken Christians who roar with the voice of God. These lions are the prayer warriors. The devil trembles at their steps, doing all he can to bully strong Christians into compliance and prayerlessness.

Although the devil flexes his muscles to flaunt his strength, he is weak. Like a lion tamer, he can be ripped to shreds by a lion that knows its dominance. The devil's only defences are fear and deception.

If he can scare or trick the Christian, he can control the Christian. And after thousands of years of telling the same lies, he has perfected just three skills: stealing, killing, and destroying (John 10:10).

God alone has the power to give life. He is omnipresent, omniscient, and omnipotent. If allowed a foothold, the enemy can oppress Christians with sorrow, fear, and pain, driving them to spiritual self-destruction or even suicide. But Jesus came that we may have life and have it more abundantly (John 10:10).

When we stay close to God, praying and reading his Word, the devil stands no chance. How can he, when Christ lives within us (Romans 8:10)? No wonder the devil works 24/7 to blind us to God's true nature. The last thing is wants is for us to recognize our authority in Christ. There is no greater weapon by which to defeat the devil than the sound of praise on our lips.

To prove his power, the devil targets the strongest, most dedicated Christians, conquering them through the art of seduction. He manipulates and influences them so subtly, they don't notice the cliff looming before of them. He attacks leaders of the biggest churches to create the biggest scandals. He is cunning, conniving, and evil. But he is also weak and cowardly. God remains the alpha, the epitome of strength. He is a force to be reckoned with. And with him beside us, so are we.

Like the lion in the circus tent, we must stand our ground to preserve our freedom. We cannot allow the tamer to subdue us, to shred our identity with the whip of lies brandished in his shaking fist. We must remember who we are: children of God and coheirs with Christ (Romans 8:17).

If you are a seasoned believer, please take time to walk hand-in-hand with new Christians. The enemy is out to steal them away, to destroy them before their faith can form a strong foundation in God's Word. Discipleship is key in defending the kingdom. The journey of a Christian is not an easy one. It invites persecution, rejection, and temptation. We must fight for each other, exhorting new believers not to give into discouragement or fall victim to lies. We must also pray for church leadership and be on our guard against the enemy as we minister to others. The devil prowls day and night.

What strengths has God given you? What lies and seductions does the devil use to whip you into submission? How can you fight your battles and defend your faith?

Day 22

He Steals, Kills, and Destroys

John 10:10

The devil seeks to destroy marriage because he fears its potential to grow maturity and sacrificial love. I love God's marital design because, through it, I learned lessons that led me on a quest to wholeness. The foundation of my marriage was shaky from the start; Christ was not the center, and I carried years of unresolved pain into the union. As equally broken people, neither my husband nor I could bear the weight of two people's baggage. We were desperate for God. Before we separated, I told my husband that if I were to do it all over again, I would pick him every time. My vows at the altar had been sincere. I was convinced I'd spend the rest of my life with my husband. However, I learned the hard way that reconciliation cannot occur without repentance (Luke 17:3). Each partner must take full responsibility for any mistakes that sabotaged the marriage.

If you and your spouse are determined to save your marriage, start by rebuilding trust through sincere repentance. The topic of marriage is complex, extending far beyond the scope of this book. For further help, contact a professional Christian counselor or support group. You can also go to my website and sign up for a coaching session. I will gladly send you resources to guide your healing journey.

Even the best marriages experience seasons of darkness. Marriage is a union between two selfish humans and, when invited, God. Both spouses are sinful, requiring a lifetime of sanctification to truly love like Christ (Philippians 1:6). While believers should certainly set biblical standards for marriage, the fact is that life is hard and people are broken. Maturation takes time. For marriage to thrive, both partners must overflow with patience, grace and forgiveness (Ephesians 4:32; 1 Corinthians 13:4-8). Each should honor the other, staying accountable to God and fellow believers (Galatians 6:1-2; Proverbs 27:17). Doing so is a powerful way to reinforce faithfulness. The seasons of marriage will ebb and flow like waves of the ocean, but with God as your anchor, your ship will not be dashed against the rocks (Isaiah 33:6; Ephesians 4:2-3).

Are you struggling to keep your marriage afloat? Have you already entered the pain of divorce? Repent and reach out for help. God is in the business of saving precarious marriages and bandaging broken hearts (Psalm 147:3).

Day 23

He Is Perverted

Acts 13:9-11

The enemy has perverted many God-given gifts, such as sex, marriage, gender, and money. All perversions are evil and blasphemous. But the most destructive perversion of all is that of the gospel. The world is filled with shelves of false gospels. This chapter will focus on one frequently peddled to poor nations by televangelists: the prosperity gospel.

Also known as the "health and wealth," "blab it and grab it," and "name it and claim it" gospel, the prosperity gospel purports that, with enough faith, a believer can download blessings on demand. One of the main issues with this belief is its focus on "me" instead of Christ. Feel-good motivational speeches leave listeners high on self but low on Christ. The prosperity gospel is a popular message that has lined the pockets of many so-called pastors—but it cannot deliver on its promises.

I grew up believing that if I had enough faith and planted a financial seed by giving money, I would receive a return in the form of material goods and health. With doubts piling up along the way, I finally questioned my faith when I lost both my best friend and my niece to cancer. I had tithed faithfully—why hadn't God healed them? And why was I still struggling financially? It seemed that God had failed to uphold his end of the bargain. My loss alerted me to the gross misconception I had accepted so blindly (Luke 12:15; James 2:5, 4:3). Suffering is a vital and guaranteed part of the Christian faith (1 Peter 5:10; Romans 5:3-5, 8:18; John 16:33). Raising a white flag, I opened my heart to receive the real truth that set me free (John 8:32).

During your healing journey, you will encounter many preachers and teachings (Matthew 24:24). You must test everything and make sure it aligns with God's Word. "Do not believe every spirit, but test the spirits to see whether they are from God, because many false prophets have gone out into the world. This is how you can recognize the Spirit of God: Every spirit that acknowledges that Jesus Christ has come in the flesh is from God, but every spirit that does not acknowledge Jesus is not from God. This is the spirit of the antichrist, which you have heard is coming and even now is already in the world" (1 John 4:1-3).

Just because a message is popular doesn't make it true. "For the time will come when people will not put up with sound doctrine. Instead, to suit their own desires, they will gather around them a great number of teachers to say what their itching ears want to hear. They will turn their ears away from the truth and turn aside to myths" (2 Timothy 4:3

You know the saying that the best lie is the one closest to the truth. Remember that. The devil perverts the truth just enough to deceive you but not enough to appear on your radar. Only mature believers who are saturated in truth are equipped to discern his lies (Hebrews 5:14). Jesus himself used Scripture to fight the enemy (Matthew 4:1-11). So study the Bible thoroughly. God's Word is the only offensive weapon we have (Ephesians 6:17).

Which gospel do you believe? Is it self-focused or God-focused? Consider this: If your gospel would not attract unbelievers to an underground church in a communist country, it's probably not the gospel Jesus preached. Repent of any false teachings you have accepted, and ask God to reveal the truth.

Day 24

The Father of Many Lies

1 John 4:4

The devil cannot read your mind. He is not all-knowing. But he has been practicing the same lies for thousands of years. Observing our patterns and weaknesses, he plants seeds of deception into our minds. If we allow them to take root, we give the devil a foothold with which to oppress us. These spiritual viruses are like the malware that sneaks onto your computer hard drive through what seems like an innocent download. Once there, it takes control of your device and corrupts your files. Likewise, the enemy's lies corrupt our minds, turning us into agents of hate toward God, ourselves, and others. They draw our focus away from God so that his loving truth falls on deaf ears and blind eyes (Isaiah 35:5).

Because Jesus paid the ultimate price for our sins, building an unbreakable bridge between us and heaven, God never leaves our side. He is always right here, right now. Although the devil deludes us into believing we're alone, the fact is that God does not abandon his children. He sees our bindings and our blindness, and he can free us (John 8:31-32). Open your heart to his truth, and he will lead you in the path of righteousness (Psalm 23:3). Reach for God, and he will reach for you (James 4:8). "Trust in the Lord with all your heart and lean not on your own understanding; in all your ways submit to him, and he will make your paths straight" (Proverbs 3:5-6).

The devil says we are weaker than he is. The Bible says we are stronger than he is. Why? Because we house the Spirit of God (1 John 4:4). The devil is a created being. And no creature in heaven or on Earth is greater than—or even comparable to—God (Psalm 113:4-6). When we speak the Word of God with love and confidence, we take authority over the devil. Our voices roar in unison with the Lion of Judah. Remember how "Judah" means "praise"? If you find yourself weighed down by the chains of guilt or shame, praise God and remind the enemy that he has no power over you. If you feel walled in by crushing waves of fear, raise your hands and let the truth of God's glory echo from the depths of your heart. Once we release the Lion inside, the devil's hold on us slips and our bondage shatters. Arm yourself with Scripture!

The perfect love of God casts out all fear (1 John 4:18). With Jesus beside us, we can face the enemy head-on, boldly commanding him out of our minds and lives. James 4:7 says, "Submit yourselves, then, to God. Resist the devil, and he will flee from you." When we flood the atmosphere with praise, the devil's kingdom shakes to the ground. The gates of hell cannot prevail against a Church that breathes such power (Matthew 16:18). You are on the offensive! If Almighty God is for us, not one can stand against us (Romans 8:31).

God is calling you to reject your sin, return home, and serve him. Submit to him now, while you still can. A time is coming like that of Noah. Sooner or later, God will once again pour out his judgment on this rebellious world. God is merciful, but he is also just. How can righteousness allow evil to reign indefinitely? How can light tolerate darkness? It is not possible. God's character cannot accept anything less than holiness. That is why a day is coming when he will purge the earth of the devil's disease. He will wipe out anyone who stands against him—just as he did in the time of Noah (Genesis 6-9). Though not in the form of a flood, God's wrath is on the horizon. But take heart. Salvation entered the world through Jesus Christ. It's yours for the taking (John 3:16).

How has the devil turned your gaze from God? What lies has he tricked you into believing? What truth does God wish to free you with? How can you turn back to God so he can break the chains binding you?

Day 25

The Great Deceiver

Genesis 3:1-3

U nfortunately, human aversion to pain and suffering is no secret to the devil (1 Peter 5:8). He uses it to trick us into believing that unpleasant feelings are something to run from or internalize. Perhaps they indicate that we don't really matter, that God has given up on us, or that we are just too broken to be fixed. Discipline is a guaranteed part of our growth as Christ's disciples (Matthew 16:24). Although it does not feel comfortable, it is the obligation of any loving parent (Proverbs 13:24). And God, being the ultimate loving parent, makes our sanctification a priority (Hebrews 12:10).

The pain and turmoil eating away at your heart is merely a reminder that you need Jesus. I used to think my suffering was punishment from God for my sins. We live in fallen world and sin has its consequences. However, there are times when we face trials that are meant to build character. This is like the pain we feel when we exercise our muscles.

In Romans 5:3-5, Paul says that we can "glory in our sufferings, because we know that suffering produces perseverance; perseverance, character; and character, hope. And hope does not put us to shame, because God's love has been poured out into our hearts through the Holy Spirit, who has been given to us." Similarly, James 1:2-4 says, "Consider it pure joy, my brothers and sisters, whenever you face trials of many kinds, because you know that the testing of your faith produces perseverance. Let perseverance finish its work so that you may be mature and complete, not lacking anything."

Pain is a good thing if it compels us to acknowledge our brokenness and dependence on God. Amid the shambles, God pours out his love. He pieces us together into beautiful vessels ready to be used for his glory. When we feel pain in our bodies, we go to the doctor. There we discover the medical problem behind the symptom. Physical pain is the body's way of alerting us that something is wrong. When we pay attention to it, we can seek treatment and, often, be healed.

The pain in our hearts and souls sometimes manifests as depression or anxiety. These spiritual symptoms warn us that something needs fixing. It could be hidden sin, festering bitterness, or any number of wounds left untreated. Sometimes neglected hurts develop into diagnosable mental health problems. Although mental illnesses can certainly pass down genetically, the bottom line is that God can break generational cycles of bondage with the power of his covenantal love (Deuteronomy 7:9). Trust in God, and he will heal you of all infirmities—if not on this side of eternity, then in heaven (Revelation 21:4). He loves you and wants to transform you through the renewal of your mind (Romans 12:1-2).

It is not uncommon for a mother to threaten her misbehaving children that, as soon as their father returns home, he will punish them. In an attempt to better control their children, people often instill unhealthy fear in them. The sad thing is that this fear is directed toward the parents who should embody love. A child raised this way grows up scared that her father is just a distant figure waiting to strike her whenever she messes up.

The devil tries the same tactic of control on us. He fills our minds with whispered threats, lying about God's character and making us doubt God's goodness (John 8:44). With pleasure at our trembling, he tricks us into believing that God is out to punish us. But God is not tapping his fingers on the arm on his throne, waiting for us to fail so he can strike us. He does not wield disease and poverty over our necks like swords of divine justice (James 1:17; Matthew 5:45).

Yes, our sins have natural consequences that God allows. But he already poured out his wrath upon Christ. All our sins were covered at the cross. We don't have to heap coals on our heads as punishment for our wrongdoings. The only thing we are called to do is repent. Once God forgives us our sins, he doesn't even remember them (Hebrews 8:12). They are as far from him as the east is from the west (Psalm 103:12).

God has given us such great freedom in Christ. We can go to our Heavenly Father and call him Abba—or Papa, as I love to say (Psalm 103:13). God does discipline us, but only to protect and lead us home (Psalm 23:2-3). He doesn't condemn us or whip our backs with guilt or shame. He guides us gently in the right path.

How do you view God? Is he a volatile punisher or a loving protector? From where does your impression come? How does it compare to the

God of the Bible? What things has God forgiven that the devil still holds against you? Is there guilt or shame that you need to let go?

Day 26

He Is Dangerous

2 Timothy 3:1-6

The Bible prophesies that, in the last days, abuse and oppression will run rampant. In 2 Timothy 3:1-9, Paul warns about the dangers ahead:

> You should know this, Timothy, that in the last days there will be very difficult times. For people will love only themselves and their money. They will be boastful and proud, scoffing at God, disobedient to their parents, and ungrateful. They will consider nothing sacred. They will be unloving and unforgiving; they will slander others and have no self-control. They will be cruel and hate what is good. They will betray their friends, be reckless, be puffed up with pride, and love pleasure rather than God. They will act religious, but they will reject the power that could make them godly. Stay away from people like that!
>
> They are the kind who work their way into people's homes and win the confidence of vulnerable women who are burdened with the guilt of sin and controlled by various desires. (Such

women are forever following new teachings, but they are never able to understand the truth.) These teachers oppose the truth just as Jannes and Jambres opposed Moses. They have depraved minds and a counterfeit faith. But they won't get away with this for long. Someday everyone will recognize what fools they are, just as with Jannes and Jambres. (NLT)

When Jesus walked the earth, he focused on liberating people from oppression of all kinds. The first sermon Jesus ever preached was about his desire to set captives free (Luke 4:18-19). He quoted the prophet Isaiah, saying, "The Spirit of the Sovereign Lord is on me, because the Lord has anointed me to proclaim good news to the poor. He has sent me to bind up the brokenhearted, to proclaim freedom for the captives and release from darkness for the prisoners" (Isaiah 61:1). If Jesus deemed freedom an important topic with which to begin his ministry, then I too must talk about oppression. Especially because I know firsthand how the human soul can be freed to embrace the abundant life God offers. Jesus came to set the captives free (Luke 4:18)!

If I truly love Jesus, I must also love pointing people to him. Once in his arms, they can be released from oppression by the transformation of their minds (Romans 12:2). God's Word is the ultimate key, able to unlock even the heaviest shackles. A powerful tool of liberation, it is banned in all communist countries. Those governments realize that the gospel of Christ can spark a revolution. While learning how to lead a revolution that would change the course of history, Dr. Martin Luther King Jr. studied Jesus. Even Gandhi, an unbeliever, used Jesus' teachings as a guide while peacefully campaigning for India's independence from British colonialists.

These heroes from history have taught me that when you walk straight with your head held high, no one can ride on your back. However, when you bend over under the weight of shame and guilt, anyone can ride on your back. And then they hijack the power that should be God's. Be alert! These are the last days. Study the Word of God. It will set you free!

What can you do to share the good news of the freedom you have found in Christ?

Day 27

He's After Your Seed

Matthew 13:1-23

There is a treasure hidden inside you. It is a seed God planted before you were even born (Psalm 139:13-14). When God formed you inside your mother's womb, he gave you everything you need. You were created whole, a beautiful reflection of God's image made to shine light into the world. Each of us is anointed for a life that exudes Christ. We are supernaturally equipped to spread hope to our families, our communities, and our planet.

Naturally, Satan is not a fan of our heavenly calling. Because he knows that the seeds we harbor are powerful enough to tear down his kingdom, he'll do whatever it takes to kill them and destroy God's vision. The brokenness flashing across the five o'clock news is evidence of the enemy's thirst for souls: rape, murder, abuse, oppression, war—the list goes on.

Living in a fallen world, we must fight daily to stay focused on God's vision for our lives. God is powerful, determined to protect his children. After all, he gave us purpose even before creating the foundation of the world (Ephesians 1:4, 2:10). In Philippians 1:6,

Paul says that, "He who began a good work in you will bring it to completion until the day of Christ Jesus."

The enemy first began hunting my seed when I was a child. Why? Because I am a warrior for Christ. Since I was a teenager, all I ever dreamed of was being a worship leader and summer camp counselor. After I got saved, my heart was on fire for God. I wanted to see everyone saved and headed toward heaven. But as I grew, the pleasures of this world distracted me, pulling my eyes away from God's plan for my life. Guarding our seeds is a daily discipline. Here's how to do it:

❖ Take time to develop a solid foundation on Christ. Know who God says you are and what your purpose is.

❖ Avoid people who belittle, bully, or misguide you.

❖ Don't enter relationships because you want only the benefits or because you're lonely.

❖ Maintain your chastity until marriage.

❖ Don't gossip or slander others.

❖ Share your vision with caution. Don't spill your precious pearls to every little piggy you meet.

❖ Guard your heart by avoiding toxic television shows, music and movies.

❖ Pray without ceasing and stay in the Word.

❖ Obey when God prompts you to do the next right thing.

❖ Limit your alcohol intake and steer clear of mind-altering drugs. Don't risk impairing your judgment and making decisions that cost more than you expect.

Think of your seed as your calling in life. It is the God-given purpose you must guard with your whole heart. If you do, it will blossom.

How can you foster the seed God's planted inside you? What are some things that threaten to dry out or steal your seed? Create a vision board and place it somewhere obvious so you stay focused on God's plan.

PART IV
Knowing the Truth

Day 28

From What Are We Saved?

Galatians 5:16-26

As a child, I understood salvation differently than I do now. At eleven, I said the Sinner's Prayer so I wouldn't go to hell. I thought all it took to avoid eternal damnation was saying some magical words and—tada! You're saved! I remember the moment I raised my hand in response to an altar call. I'd just attended a Heaven's Gates and Hell's Flames theater production at my local church. I don't doubt that I was truly saved that day, but I've come to realize that salvation is more than just casting a spell or responding to an altar call. When I surrendered my life to God this last year, it felt a lot like being resurrected from the dead.

To accept salvation means to become saved from the curse of Adam and Eve's sin. Jesus saved me from the pursuit of things that bring fleeting satisfaction and permanent death. I can now pursue God with the same passion I once had for worldly things. All my hope is found in Christ. Salvation is an instantaneous event that takes place the moment we accept Christ and sanctification is a continuous process of spiritual refinement. I die to myself daily, pick up my cross daily, and give up my fleshly desires daily. I seek God with every heartbeat, pursuing him as if Christ is the only thing worth living for—which he is. I am dead to my flesh and alive in him. The Holy Spirit lives within me, empowering me to live a pure and holy life. It is no longer I who live but Christ who lives in me. The less there is of my sinful nature, the more there is of his perfect one (John 3:30).

I am saved from the consequence of sin that is death, baptized forever into the kingdom of God. Righteousness, peace, and joy overflowing from the Holy Spirit—that's salvation. It is not by my own strength that I boast, but by God's grace, by the blood he shed on the cross for me. At the cross, I find freedom and healing. It is where Jesus set me free. Fear no longer has a hold on me. My identity is in Christ. There is no other hope, no alternative salvation from humanity's curse. Jesus said, "I am the way and the truth and the life. No one comes to the Father except through me" (John 14:6). This is the gospel that so many have given their lives for. Now it's our honor to do the same (Romans 14:8).

What do you need saving from? What are some habits that you just can't seem to shake? What new behaviors and traits do you desire? How can you start dying to self and living for God?

Day 29

You Can Be Free

1 John 2:15-16

Mental slavery is an insidious form of Satan's bondage. Until Jesus sets you free, the following three landmines are guaranteed to keep you trapped in a state of modern-day slavery: the pride of life, the lust of the flesh, and the lust of the eyes. No created thing can satisfy the human soul. Nothing. The wisest man to ever live, other than Christ, was King Solomon. He had more wealth, power, women, and insight than anyone else on Earth—yet he was still not satisfied. If we look to things of this world for fulfillment, we will be disappointed. In Ecclesiastes 1:14, the wise king denounces his futile lifestyle: "I have seen all the things that are done under the sun; all of them are meaningless, a chasing after the wind."

Young people who discover sex at an early age often become intoxicated by the pleasure, dedicating their lives to pursuit of a temporary high, but never capturing it for longer than a few fleeting seconds. There is no human being on Earth able to fully meet your every need. Not even your spouse. You can search eternally, jumping from one relationship to the next, but will never find the permanent satisfaction you're desperate for. King Solomon, who had everything a man could dream of, deemed it all worthless (Ecclesiastes 1:2). There is a God-shaped hole in your soul. And the only one who can fill it is Jesus.

What temporary distractions do you use to fill the hole in your heart? Is your soul truly satisfied? Ask God to break your mind free of its shackles, clear away the enemy's clutter, and fill your spiritual void with himself.

Day 30

Breath of Life

Matthew 6:33

I can't survive a single day without my wakeup hour of power. Morning time with God is the oxygen I need to keep breathing. Oxygen makes up only 21 percent of the air in Earth's atmosphere, with the other 79 percent comprising various gases. Despite its low percentage, however, oxygen is vital to our survival. Relationship with God is the soul's oxygen. Substitute it with something else, and we suffocate spiritually. Human relationships are like the other gases. Though they take up about 80 percent of our time and energy, they do not offer salvation. The only relationship a healthy soul cannot live without is a personal, intimate one with Jesus. He is the breath of life.

God created us with a need for him. He did so to ensure that we never cease fellowship. When we ignore him, we start to experience the symptoms of spiritual suffocation: anxiety, fear, depression, anger, bitterness, frustration, and instability. These negative effects are signs of a void only God can fill. Pursue God first thing after waking up. Morning devotion offers a sacred time to inhale the oxygen our souls need for the day. My calculations suggest that 20 percent of my active day equals about two hours. That means I should spend at least a couple of hours meditating on God. I can spend the remaining eight on other things that are glorifying to him. Allotting my time this way keeps me positive and motivated to walk in truth. It's hard but worth it!

It's when we hit rock bottom that we realize how much we need God daily—not just on Sundays. The devil is out to get us every minute of every day. A mere moment of loneliness or pain can tempt us to self-soothe with things like alcohol, drugs, sex, pornography, binge eating, or T.V. When we start to drift away from God, the enemy pounces, heaping mountains of guilt and shame in our tracks to distance us permanently. But God is a good Father; he always rescues us. When you hear that still, small voice whisper for you to return to fellowship with Christ, don't ignore it. Allow God to bring you back home. Once there, dive into disciplined prayer and meditation on God's Word. Devotion must be a constant flow of oxygen. Don't push away the clean air, or you will inhale toxins. Breathe in the pure oxygen of God's fellowship, and you will never suffocate again.

"Everyone who calls on the name of the Lord will be saved" (Romans 10:13). When you fall away from God and find yourself clutching at the frayed end of your rope, you can call upon the Lord to rescue you. If you're dizzy from breathing poisonous air, desperate for the smallest gasp of oxygen, he will fill your lungs. God abounds with second, third, and fourth chances.

What relationships, behaviors, or things do you breathe in place of oxygen? What is their effect on your spiritual health? If you are suffering from spiritual suffocation, what can you do to breathe again?

Day 31

We Are All Lost

Luke 15:11-32

Contrary to popular belief, the parable of the prodigal son is not about only one lost son. It is about two: a younger one who left home to squander his inheritance and an older one who stayed home to fulfil his duties. Despite living with his father and enjoying the gifts regularly showered on him, the older brother had no intimate relationship with him. Jesus used this metaphor to expose the pharisees. They too valued God's blessings over his person, clinging to their inheritance and shutting out his heart. In the parable, the older brother didn't need to toil in the field or work as a servant to please his father. He could have feasted at the table with him instead, sharing life together as daddy and son. Instead, he chose to act as a slave—all in an attempt to keep up the appearance of a "good" son.

When the younger son returned home after reducing himself to squalor, his father dressed him in fine clothes and ordered the fattened calf be killed for a feast (Luke 15:22-23). But instead of joining in the celebration, the older brother complained. He pouted that his father never threw *him* a party to enjoy with his friends—and he was the good son! "All I have is yours!" his father responded.

After all, he'd distributed his wealth equally between his two sons. Whatever the father had belonged to them. Unlike the older son, the father desired relationship far more than he did any worldly possession. He longed to be close, to feast with his children daily. But the older son was not interested.

Picture the father: an elderly man sitting alone at the table every day, waiting hopefully for his sons to join him. He spends his evenings peering into the distance for a glimpse of his younger son returning home. Then one day, it finally happens. The father is filled with joy—his son is home at last! Tonight, they will dine together. He runs towards his beloved son, so overcome with love that he loses all dignity and falls on his neck, kissing him repeatedly. The father doesn't wait for his son to repent or explain why his clothes are so tattered, why he smells so bad. He has no wish to dwell on his son's downcast spirit. Instead, he instantly instructs his servants to dress his son with the finest robe, comfortable shoes, and a signet ring to signify his sonship. The father finally has his son back. This evening, and for many more evenings to come, they can eat at the table together.

At the sound of music and dancing, the older son returns from the field and learns that his younger brother has come home. When his father invites him to join the celebration, he walks away, grieved by his father's acceptance of his wayward brother.

Jesus' parable raises this question: who is the lost son? The answer is both. While one returned, the other remained lost. The older son represents the pharisees who spent their entire lives in the synagogue but kept their hearts far from the love of God. Such people are like whitewashed tombs. Jesus came to set us free from the bondage of works-based religion, inviting us instead to grace-based relationship. Will you accept his invitation to dine together?

Which brother do you relate to most? Is it possible that you see yourself in both? In what ways do you identify with the older brother? How can you let appearances go and accept your Heavenly Father's invitation to a lifetime of daddy-daughter dates?

Day 32

You ARE Forgiven

Psalm 51

How could I have been so horrible? Why did I mess up so bad?"

Questions like these often play on loop in the mind of a contrite Christian. Initially, shame acts as a catalyst, propelling us toward repentance and grace. It is not uncommon, however, for the mental tape to continue playing long after God forgives us. Oddly, the closest thing to relief we can find comes from perpetually beating ourselves up. This behavior of latching onto past sins raises the question: Should we forgive ourselves?

If you feel like you're drowning in a river of past wrongs, frantically treading water that should be miles under the bridge, let me throw you a rope: the Bible mentions no gospel of self-forgiveness. The true anchor pulling you down is Satan—or, more specifically, his unrelenting accusation and condemnation (Revelation 12:10).

When we ask God for forgiveness, we must trust in the power of the death and resurrection of Christ to save us, to expunge all guilt and shame from our souls, and to set us free from the past. "For God did not send his Son into the world to condemn the world, but to save the world through him. Whoever believes in him is not condemned, but whoever does not believe stands condemned already because they have not believed in the name of God's one and only Son" (John 3:17-18). If self-forgiveness were possible, the cross would not be necessary.

Only two types of forgiveness appear in the Bible: forgiveness from God and forgiveness from others. When we sin against God, we must apologize sincerely and ask him to forgive us (1 John 1:9). Likewise, when we sin against others, we must apologize and ask them to forgive us (James 5:16). It doesn't matter how much time has passed since the offense; confessing sin brings healing. This principle extends also to finances. Debt can be crushing. Growing heavier the longer we carry it, the weight is released from our shoulders only when it is met or erased. If we are unable to pay a debt, we should humbly confess to the lender and seek forgiveness. Otherwise, our silence invites guilt and shame to gnaw at our core. Can self-forgiveness truly soothe this regret? Not according to the Bible. There is no sense in attempting to forgive ourselves for crimes we've committed against others. The only people with the right (and duty) to forgive us are our victims—not us.

What a relief! This truth should lift a heavy weight from our shoulders. As Christians, our sole responsibility is that of offering a penitent heart. Forgiveness is up to others. If people refuse to forgive us, that is their problem to hash out with the Lord. Since forgiveness of sin comes ultimately from God, we can take comfort in the knowledge that we obeyed his command to seek forgiveness and reconciliation. The past is in the past. Let it go.

Easier said than done, right? Do you ever wonder when the "feeling" of forgiveness will kick in? Sometimes, no matter how hard we shake, that nagging leech called regret just refuses to fall off. So let's look to the Bible for an example of God's forgiveness in action. David committed adultery and murder. As a man after God's own heart, he was deeply convicted of his sin (1 Samuel 13:14). He recognized his sin as an offense, chiefly, toward God (Psalm 51:4). David's prayer of repentance beautifully models the way Christians should ask God for forgiveness (Psalm 51:7-15, NLT):

> Purify me from my sins, and I will be clean;
> wash me, and I will be whiter than snow.
> Oh, give me back my joy again;
> you have broken me—
> now let me rejoice.
> Don't keep looking at my sins.
> Remove the stain of my guilt.
> Create in me a clean heart, O God.
> Renew a loyal spirit within me.
> Do not banish me from your presence,
> and don't take your Holy Spirit from me.
>
> Restore to me the joy of your salvation,
> and make me willing to obey you.
> Then I will teach your ways to rebels,
> and they will return to you.
> Forgive me for shedding blood, O God who saves;
> then I will joyfully sing of your forgiveness.
> Unseal my lips, O Lord,
> that my mouth may praise you.

When we ask God to forgive us, he does! Believe it and rejoice! Praise him, celebrate his unconditional forgiveness, and embrace your freedom: "Therefore, there is now no condemnation for those who are in Christ Jesus, because through Christ Jesus the law of the Spirit who gives life has set you free from the law of sin and death" (Romans 8:1). If you have made the decision to follow Jesus and believe he died to forgive you of your sins, you can throw the shackles off. Yes, you will still give in to temptation and fleshly desire sometimes. But remember, "if we confess our sins, he is faithful and just and will forgive us our sins and purify us from all unrighteousness" (1 John 1:9). When you find yourself caving to the enemy's continual condemnation of forgiven sin, don't waste time worrying about self-forgiveness. Ask God to revive your heart with the joy of salvation and to renew your spirit. He will make your cup run over so you can't help but praise him (Psalm 23:5). There is no feeling of forgiveness like that which comes from the recognition that we are, truly, free (Psalm 103:12).

Are you stealing from your future by paying for past mistakes with self-hatred? God wants you to let go. If you need forgiveness from someone, ask for it. Don't worry about how long ago you committed the offense. If the person has passed away, write a letter and confess to God.

Day 33

He Is Light

Isaiah 60:1-3

" A rise, shine, for your light has come, and the glory of the Lord rises upon you. See, darkness covers the earth and thick darkness is over the peoples, but the Lord rises upon you and his glory appears over you. Nations will come to your light, and kings to the brightness of your dawn" (Isaiah 60:1-3).

A candle burns brightest in total darkness. Muted by competing sources of light and melted by passing time, it is unsustainable. Its effect is only temporary. Before Jesus entered my life and lit up my world, I was living in total darkness. Buried under religious rules, I could barely see all the growth my character still needed. I went through the motions of obeying the Ten Commandments, but legalism and self-righteous pride deadened my soul. When Jesus rescued me, his love illuminated my life like a sunrise. Brilliant light flooding the horizon of my heart, I welcomed the golden rays of Christ's grace. His new covenant is warm and bright, radiating energy to sustain life. When the Son is shining, there is no need for a candle. Jesus' light fulfills the old testament law.

Modern-day pharisees carry a candle of legalism everywhere they go, waving it around as a reminder to follow the rules—but when the love of Jesus starts to shine, that candle dwindles to a shadow in comparison. God wants us to exude his kind of light. We can do so by obeying his two great instructions: Love God with all your heart, soul, mind, and strength, and love your neighbor as yourself (Matthew 22:36-40). Together, they are perfect. Apart from these two commandments, there is no law. God did not come to eradicate the law but to fulfill it (Matthew 5:17).

Jesus gives us something brighter than candles. On Earth, he preached about the free gift of eternal life and unlimited access to the Father's love. The old law served a purpose, and the pharisees loved wielding it to satiate their need for power. But Jesus offered a greater commandment, one that would fulfill the Old Testament law: The law of love for God and others. Life in the Spirit is freeing, requiring only faith and not works (Ephesians 2:8-9; Galatians 2:16; Romans 3:28). It overflows with righteousness, joy, and peace. Legalism, on the other hand, crushes people under its weight (Galatians 3:10-14). Those who continue to live according to the law and, thus, their own flesh are full of fear, suspicion, misery, and bitterness. Yet all they have to do is flip the switch from law to love. Often, people are afraid to turn on the light because they know its glory will expose the hidden sins lurking in dark corners of their hearts.

Someone who lives in a candlelit home cannot see the dusty surfaces begging for a good clean. If we choose to live in spiritual darkness with nothing but a candle, how can we possibly deep-clean our souls? We are blind to our own sins. That's why Jesus called the pharisees whitewashed tombs (Matthew 23:27-28). Although they feigned holiness, they were far from holy. Because we are not unlike the pharisees, God asks us to flip the switch and allow Christ's light to shine. Only then can we clearly see the dust and grime coating our souls. If we get our hands dirty alongside Jesus, we can clear out the muck of unrepented sin. Together, we can finally toss the trash that's been rotting in our hearts for years, oozing the stench of bitterness and anger.

Allow Christ to enter your heart, and he will illuminate your life and fill you with the Holy Spirit. Equipped with the power to defeat the enemy, you can retire your legalism candle and step out of the darkness. Arise, shine—the Light has come (John 8:12).

Accepting Jesus is the only way to defeat the cycle of sin that keeps us in bondage. To embrace salvation means to walk in the light of truth. A lifelong process of purging the junk from our hearts, sanctification is a journey toward righteousness (2 Timothy 2:21). At its end stands the doorway to eternal life with God. It takes considerable work and reflection to walk in truth. Jesus warned that many will fall by the wayside or be enticed to easier paths: "Enter through the narrow gate. For wide is the gate and broad is the road that leads to destruction, and many enter through it. But small is the gate and narrow the road that leads to life, and only a few find it" (Matthew 7:13-14). Choose the path less traveled and leave a trail of light.

Do you ever catch yourself waving a legalism candle when you should be radiating Christ's light? If so, consider your motives. What hidden sins has God's light exposed? How does he want you to deal with them?

Confess and repent so you can receive forgiveness. Ask God to help you turn from your actions and walk in surrender and truth.

PART V
Knowing Your Purpose

Day 34

Come As You Are

1 Corinthians 1:26–31

D
o you sometimes feel like you are way too flawed to serve in church? Perhaps you feel that those who are actively preaching the gospel are not as broken and damaged as you are. Maybe you've already declared yourself as damaged goods and not fit for the work of ministry. If you're waiting for the moment when your relationship is right with God and you feel holy enough to serve, you will never get there.

When Jesus calls you to serve, he will accept you just as you are. Paul was called into ministry on his way to persecuting Christians (Acts 9:1-31). God called me to preach the Gospel in the same year that marriage fell apart, my heart was broken and I had nothing to give other than my ashes. But with those ashes, God is molding me and shaping me into a vessel that is fit for his use. He reminded me that, although I may be rejected by humans, I am still accepted by God. We can never please everyone. No matter how perfect we try to be, someone will always find a reason to reject us.

Jesus *is* perfect. Yet even he was hated and rejected. His goodness did not automatically cause everyone to love him. Because I've always sought the approval of others, this realization came as a wakeup call. Jesus set me free to live for an audience of one: God. His approval far outweighs the opinions of other fallible humans.

Jesus, in his loving kindness and grace, has invited me to walk humbly with God. With him, I am totally vulnerable, poignantly aware of my flawed human nature. I am a sinner who desperately needs a Savior. The only righteousness I can put on is Christ's. Without his wings of grace covering me, I am nothing. And that's the best news a broken-down Christian can hear. I don't need perfection or a fairytale life to be worthy of sharing the gospel. My testimony has the most power when I own who I am: a single mother, wounded, neglected, rejected, and—yes—divorced. These labels do not describe a status likely to launch me into ministry. But God uses the most unexpected things to exemplify his unfailing forgiveness and redemptive love. God chooses people the world deems foolish to shame those the world deems wise. He chooses the powerless to shame the powerful (1 Corinthians 1:27).

God does not call the qualified; he qualifies those he calls. I am honored and humbled by his desire to use me in even the smallest ways, given my many flaws and heavy baggage. However, it is God's nature to repurpose broken vessels. With gentle hands, he molds them and fills the cracks with gold, refining them so they can carry his love to a hurting world. I have been through the fire, crushed by trials and suffering. But in the midst of the crucible, God welded my soul back together. I am stronger today thanks to the pain I have endured and the Savior who loved me through it.

When we replace self-righteousness with God's righteousness, we can reach out to others with authenticity. Yes, it takes immense vulnerability to unveil past darkness and sins. It takes even more to expose current darkness and sins. But dying to self in this way opens many more ears to the gospel. People want to hear from Christians they can relate to. When we present ourselves as self-made saints, we invite listeners to accuse us of being hypocrites—and rightly so. People have a way of digging up dirt! Only Jesus, who was fully God and fully man, lived a sinless life. We, on the other hand are in the process of being sanctified.

Sanctification is a lifelong process of becoming like Christ. But it is also a one-time event already completed by God. We were fully sanctified, or set apart, when Christ died and rose again. When God looks at a repentant believer, he sees perfection. Why? Because in front of the sinner stands Christ. Yet sanctification is also a journey. In this very moment, we are being cleansed. And one day, we will experience the righteousness that is already a reality in God's eyes. The Bible calls Christians to walk daily in the forgiveness God extended through the cross. We must confess, repent, and surrender to God until the day we die. On that day, we will fully embody Christ. But until then, our souls need cleansing.

You are a child of God. Don't write yourself off because you have a gritty past. Remember my story. I was once lonely, broken, empty, lost, sinful, controlling, prideful, lustful, shameful, fearful, needy, and rejected. But God is transforming me. He calls me chosen, redeemed, adopted, saved, whole, found, righteous, holy, accepted, loved, courageous, prayer warrior, blameless, and justified. By the power of the risen Christ, I can claim a new identity. Not because I deserve it, but because he paid dearly for my redemption. "God made him who had no sin to be sin for us, so that in him we might become the righteousness of God" (2 Corinthians 5:21).

Write out your testimony, including the parts that are not so pretty. How did God redeem you? Try sharing the tough chapters of your story to nudge another broken soul toward Jesus.

Day 35

Feed My Sheep

John 21:1-17

"**D**o you love me?" This is the question that Jesus asked Peter three times in John 21:15-17. Why? Didn't he already know the answer? Yes. But he wanted Peter to reflect on his own heart. How passionate was his desire, how deep his longing for Jesus? We must ask ourselves the same question. Do we love Jesus? If the answer is yes, he offers the same response he gave Peter: "Feed my sheep." But what exactly does that mean? In the Great Commission, Jesus instructs us to go out into the world and make disciples—not just fans (Matthew 28:19-20).

Let's look at the moments leading up to Jesus' question. After his resurrection, Jesus appears on the shore of the Sea of Galilee, where he finds Peter and six friends fishing. After working all night, they have caught nothing. Peter is overjoyed to see Jesus alive, but his betrayal of Jesus still haunts him (Luke 22:54-62). Knowing that Peter is afraid his triple denial has disqualified him from discipleship, Jesus assures him three times that the calling still stands: Feed my sheep! We often assume that our brokenness disqualifies us from our purpose, but it doesn't. Forgiveness and restoration compel us to fulfill the Great Commission.

Jesus called Peter to discipleship the very first time they met. Instead of being a fisherman, Peter would become a fisher of men (Matthew 4:19). So why did he return to his old ways? Humans often park themselves on benches that are comfortable and familiar instead of braving unknown paths that are challenging and rewarding. Jesus went to the Sea of Galilee to remind Peter of his new identity in Christ. God's great plan for Peter had not changed: "On this rock I will build my church, and the gates of Hades will not overcome it" (Matthew 16:18b). Peter's deep love for Christ meant he had an assignment to fulfill. But, Jesus explained, the road would not be easy. He warned Peter of the immense suffering to come. He even foretold Peter's horrific death. But it had to be done—the gospel must be shared with all people. Because Jesus knew that the disciples couldn't manage such a hefty task on their own, he instructed them to stay in Jerusalem until he sent the Holy Spirit (Acts 1:4). On the day of Pentecost, they would be empowered to preach the gospel and perform many signs and wonders (Acts 2:43).

Peter without the Holy Spirit was just a normal guy going through the motions of a mundane life: wake up, fish with the buddies, sleep, repeat. But Peter with the Holy Spirit housed the power to change the world. Imagine if the seven disciples from John 21 had decided to loiter on the shore, chatting idly about the three amazing years they'd spent with Jesus. What if they'd returned to everyday life and left the gospel trapped in memories? We Christians do exactly that when we cower in our church bubble, never venturing beyond the comfort of small Bible study groups. This apathetic habit feeds only ourselves. Jesus called us to feed his lost sheep. If we love Christ, we must go out into the dark, grungy parts of the world and preach the gospel. By dying to self, we can offer a starving society the permanent solution to its never-ending hunger: the living Word of God. "Therefore, go and make disciples of all nations, baptizing them in the name of the Father and of the Son and of the Holy Spirit" (Matthew 28:19).

Do you remember hearing the gospel for the first time? How did it feel to have your spiritual hunger finally satiated? How can you bring others that same hope? Write out a gospel message for a close friend who needs encouragement today.

Day 36

Nothing Left but Everything

Matthew 15:29-39

On my way home from work one day, I stopped at 7-Eleven for some gas. Something caught my eye as I pulled into the lot. A haggard woman was rummaging through the trash for cans and bottles. My heart brimmed with compassion. Stepping from my car, I asked the woman if she was collecting those things to sell for food money. She said yes. I told her I would top her off with $10, which she very much appreciated. Curious about her story and wishing to help in a more meaningful way, I offered some words of encouragement. I then asked if she was homeless. As she nodded, she explained that her tent was one of many pitched along the riverbank. An entire community lived in her situation, trying desperately to survive each day. And there I was, with nothing but a measly $10 bill to offer.

In my heart, I knew that the greatest gift I could give her was that of God's love and salvation. I assured her that, even when circumstances make it seem like God is indifferent to our pain, he cares beyond measure. He wants to heal the damage other people have inflicted on our souls and to forgive the wrongs we ourselves have done. The woman confided that people had been cruel to her lately. She didn't understand how they could be so calloused. I replied that we live in a fallen world full of broken people. God nudged me to share my own struggle to find a home for me and my son.

Seeing that my troubles, though unpleasant, paled in comparison to her truly frightening ones, I asked the significant question: "Are you confident and secure in your relationship with God?" "Yes," she answered, without hesitation. "I know God loves me. There's a card in my tent that says 'If you were to die today, would you go to heaven?' I know I'll be with God in heaven when I die."

Tears were welling in my eyes at this point. I was overwhelmed. How could someone in her position cling so faithfully to God's love? As I contemplated, the woman told me how a mountain lion had mauled her cat of 15 years. She was heartbroken. Her cat had been her only child. She had nothing left. And yet she still trusted the goodness of God.

I thought about my own son and how blessed I am to have him. We do life together, riding the highs and lows as a team. Uphill battles feel less steep with a little companion by my side. I remember his early years that overlapped the tumultuous upheaval of my own life. Those were the days when all my energy went to caring for him in the midst of the storm. My son was the joy that pushed me through my loneliness. The pain of neglect, poverty, and constant degradation became more bearable when we were wrapped in each other's arms. My baby boy was a gift from heaven, his laughter a ray of sunshine breaking through my grief. He gave me the courage to finally take the terrifying leap: leaving my toxic marriage and starting afresh. Although my son was the catalyst toward healing, Jesus was the Savior who ultimately resurrected and restored me. I owe him my life.

Do you feel completely drained of time, energy and money and feel that you have nothing to offer? Remember, God's power is made perfect in your weakness (2 Corinthians 12:9).

Day 37

Be Fruitful, Then Multiply

John 15:1-8

In Genesis 1:28, God gives the first ever instruction to humanity: Be fruitful and multiply. In fulfilling that commission, we must consider the order of tasks. God, whose every word embodies wisdom, put fruitfulness before multiplication. That is because fruitfulness is the vital first step. When we produce good fruit, we pass it to the next generation and fill the earth with disciples of Christ. The more people who walk according to the Spirit and proclaim the gospel, the better. If we first raise our children in God's truth, it follows naturally that they will themselves draw people to Jesus. Thus, the kingdom multiplies exponentially through our fruitfulness. People without biological children can mentor spiritual sons and daughters. Although I birthed only one son, I have many sons and daughters who call me their spiritual mother. I love it!

But what does God do with trees that fail to produce fruit? In Mark 21:19, Jesus curses a barren fig tree. He doesn't do so because he's having a bad day. Every tree that does not produce good fruit will be cut down and thrown into the fire (Matthew 3:10) Jesus went even further, saying, "I am the true vine, and my Father is the gardener.

He cuts off every branch in me that bears no fruit, while every branch that does bear fruit he prunes so that it will be even more fruitful" (John 15:1-2). Bearing good fruit is a priority to God. What is good fruit? "But the fruit of the Spirit is love, joy, peace, forbearance, kindness, goodness, faithfulness, gentleness and self-control. Against such things there is no law" (Galatians 5:22-23). Jesus made clear that the world identifies his disciples by the love they show each other (John 13:35). Go out and share the Word of God. Tell everyone of his saving grace so that they too can walk in love and freedom.

Producing fruit is a big deal. Love is a big deal! So be fruitful first, and then you will multiply.

Are you producing fruit? Is it bad or good? How do you know? What fruit would you like the Holy Spirit to add to your spiritual branches? What defects would you like him to prune?

Day 38

A Shared Vision

Proverbs 29:18

My life mission became clear in 2019, 40 days before I turned 40. I could finally articulate the reason why God placed me on Earth. This new ability gave me the most liberating and satisfying feeling I've ever had. All along, God has been guiding me, laying out the path I should follow. Sometimes I disobeyed and bulldozed my way off cliffs, but God always put me safely back on track. One thing I know is that my calling involves rescuing people from slavery. God has sparked passion in my heart to walk one-on-one with people, discipling and guiding them through their journeys to healing. He has also equipped me to champion the rights of children living in Kenyan orphanages. I spoke with several people about this burden hoping to gain some support but it would take at least a year for me to discover that God has already been moving and orchestrating a huge plan to reunite children with their families.

My heart breaks for the thousands of children across the globe who are growing up in institutions rather than in families. Because I volunteered at a government-run home in Kenya, I can testify that many of these children live in prison-like conditions. Yes, they have food, clothes, a roof over their heads. But they are also prone to neglect, abuse, and other negative experiences that risk potentially irreversible physical and psychological damage. I hear their cry for freedom from this modern-day slavery. I pray that each child has the chance to be embraced by a loving family—be it through reunification, fostering, or adoption. I pray that all children find somewhere to call home and someone to love them properly.

I envision a Kenya in which all people have the right to freely pursue their God-given dreams. I envision a Kenya in which every child has access to community resources, through faith-based organizations, the local library, wild-animal parks, and more. Kenya is a beautiful country. The children should enjoy it. They have the same right to the outside air as we do. Most of us can enjoy a stroll along the beach or through the park on a whim. But our little ones are trapped within the confines of a small compound. They have no idea that a whole world lies beyond the concrete walls—a world just waiting for them to break free and explore. These children live in slavery. America alone has enough money and resources to gift an impoverished mother the opportunity to keep her children. Without help, desperation yanks them from her arms, forcing her to sacrifice her living heart to a sterile institute.

The good news is that God hears the cry of our children. I was encouraged to learn about an organization called 1MillionHome that is transforming orphanages into family reunification centers and bringing one million children back home. Home is where children have the best opportunity to thrive. Before I knew that God is working through such organizations, I was burdened by the thought that I might have to start something brand new. I often felt lonely because it seemed no one else shared my same vision. How wrong I was. I am amazed by God.

What are you passionate about? What are your gifts, spiritual or otherwise? How has God used them to advance his kingdom in the past? How would you like to see him use them in the future?

Day 39

The Blessing of Burdens

Matthew 25:14-30

D oes your heart ever break for a hurting people group or just cause? The ache you feel is a sign that Jesus' own compassion is coursing through your veins. Because God is love and his Holy Spirit lives in us, each believer carries a burden for the world. The corruption and injustice that break God's heart also break ours. God grieves for the poor, the orphans, the widows, and the homeless. He cares for his natural world and instructs us to protect it. All creation matters to him. Not even the life of a sparrow goes unnoticed (Matthew 10:29).

In Matthew 25, Jesus told his Parable of the Talents. In the story, a man entrusts three servants with his wealth before embarking on a long journey (Matthew 25:14-15). To each he gives a significant portion of money, measured in New Testament "talents," to invest wisely. With this introduction, Jesus alluded to the near future; only three chapters later, he would entrust his disciples with the same work God had given him (Matthew 28:19-20). Jesus wished to prepare them for his ascension into heaven and to burden them with his own heart for this broken world. Jesus cares about freeing captives, healing the sick, protecting orphans and widows, and housing the homeless—but most importantly, he cares about saving lost souls from eternal damnation. Once we embrace Jesus' burden, we are compelled by his Spirit to invite others into relationship with him. The longing to see them in heaven burns within us.

Let's return to the parable. In it, the master gives the first servant five talents, the second servant two, and the third servant only one—each according to his ability (Matthew 25:15). In real life, Jesus trusted Peter with the greatest burden: "And I tell you that you are Peter, and on this rock I will build my church, and the gates of Hades will not overcome it" (Matthew 16:18). What a burden and privilege to be the disciple upon which Jesus chose to build his Church! God's heaviest burdens often dovetail his highest purposes.

Consider the end of the parable. When the master returns from his trip, he asks his servants to produce the result of their work. The first two present double the talents they began with. Overjoyed at their investment, the master commends them. "Well done, good and faithful servant!" he says to each. "You have been faithful with a few things; I will put you in charge of many things. Come and share your master's happiness! " (Matthew 25:19-23)

The third servant, however, exposes a sinful attitude. He tells his master, "I knew that you are a hard man, harvesting where you have not sown and gathering where you have not scattered seed. So I was afraid and went out and hid your gold in the ground. See, here is what belongs to you" (Matthew 25:24-25). He then presents the single talent entrusted to him. The master condemns the servant as wicked and lazy, rebuking him for not depositing the talent at the bank to collect interest (Matthew 25:26-27). God looks at the heart.

The servant's sinful heart was laid bare when he pointed a finger at his master. Christians fall into the same trap when we question the sovereignty and wisdom of God. We let our doubts fester until we too point our fingers: *You don't know what it's like for humans to suffer on Earth while you sit on a throne and allow evil to ravage good people. You must not know what you're doing. Or maybe you don't care. If I were God, I wouldn't just watch passively as the world falls apart.*

Because the third servant was driven by fear and mistrust, he hid his talent. I also have allowed fear of man to bury my God-given purpose. Afraid of ridicule, judgment, persecution, and rejection, I hid my light under a bushel (Luke 11:33). Standing up to oppressive leaders is scary. Speaking out against injustice is risky. We are scared of losing our possessions, reputations, or even lives in the line of duty. Anxiety clouds our minds, and makes us wonder if God will honor his promise to stay by our side no matter what (Joshua 1:9).

The truth is that following Jesus *can* cost everything (Luke 14:33). On that point, Jesus was frank: "'Whoever wants to be my disciple must deny themselves and take up their cross and follow me" (Mark 8:34-35). But we must weigh the temporary costs against the eternal one. "For whoever wants to save their life will lose it, but whoever loses their life for me and for the gospel will save it. What good is it for someone to gain the whole world, yet forfeit their soul?'" (Mark 8:34-26) As God's children, we can trust our heavenly Father to take care of us (Matthew 6:26). If he calls us, he will provide the tools needed to fulfill our purpose (Exodus 4:11-12).

God continues to give clear instructions to this day. Some of the modern-day warriors I look up to are Joan of Arc, Harriet Tubman, William Wilberforce, Mother Theresa, Martin Luther King Jr., and Wangari Maathai. God gave all a burden, and all worked hard to accomplish his vision. Because these heroes sacrificed everything they had, elevating the well-being of others above their own, God used them to change the world. Because they multiplied the gifts God gave them, many souls met Christ. Likewise, our own heavenly potential expands when we accept Jesus' burden of love into our hearts. What will you do with your talents?

What is your burden? Do you have more than one? Do you ever brainstorm ways to help a vulnerable population or meaningful cause? If you think you've stumbled upon a solution to a stubborn problem, get out there and try it. You have an opportunity to make a difference. It doesn't matter how big or small. A simple answer could be the answer to someone's complex problem.

Day 40

Moving Forward with Purpose

Philippians 3:7-21

To forget the past and move forward doesn't mean to experience a sudden onset of amnesia. It means that, despite the shadows of yesterday, you now walk in the light. No longer programmed to self-destruct, you know better than to rehash old wounds or to spiral back into dysfunction. You see your life from a fresh perspective, one marked by wisdom and joy. Uncomfortable facts are now balanced by biblical truth. If the fact is that you are single and lonely, you choose to focus on the truth: God is with you, he loves you, and he will never leave you (Deuteronomy 31:6). If the fact is that you are unemployed, with no idea what the future holds, you choose to focus on the truth: God has already drawn up the roadmap of your life, and it leads to peace and hope (Jeremiah 29:11).

Moving forward means turning off the "if only" record your mind has played on loop for years. You know the one. It's the tune we all sing to soothe ourselves after giving up on a calling. *If only I wasn't molested. If only I were wealthy. If only I weren't divorced. If only I hadn't messed up. If only I wasn't abused. If only life had been easier.* And on it goes. Want to move forward? Shatter the record. No more excuses.

It's time to take out the emotional trash. By fixing our eyes on Christ, the author and perfector of our faith, we can reframe tough circumstances with joy Hebrews 12:2). Suffering produces perseverance, then character, then hope—and the love of God gives us every reason to hope (Romans 5:3-5).

Paul, the self-proclaimed chief of sinners, wrote, "Brothers and sisters, I do not consider myself yet to have taken hold of [perfection]. But one thing I do: Forgetting what is behind and straining toward what is ahead, I press on toward the goal to win the prize for which God has called me heavenward in Christ Jesus" (Philippians 3:13

- ❖ Forgive those who have hurt you, but take your time. Healing is a process.

- ❖ Own up to your shortcomings and repent.

- ❖ Study God's Word daily. The truth will set you free.

- ❖ Cultivate a personal relationship with God.

- ❖ Connect with a church that will nurture your faith.

- ❖ Work with a peer support group, life coach, pastor, or licensed Christian therapist.

"Therefore, as God's chosen, holy and dearly loved, clothe yourself with compassion, kindness, humility, gentleness and patience. Bear with each other and forgive one another if any of you has a grievance against someone. Forgive as the Lord forgave you" (Colossians 3:12-13).

Congratulations! You've made it through the final chapter. God has brought you far in the last 40 days. But the healing journey doesn't end here. Think about your next steps. How can you throw away your emotional trash and move forward? Are you ready for new adventures with God?

Final Words

Give like you're not afraid of running out.

Fight like you're not afraid to die.

Love like you're not afraid of getting hurt.

Sing like you're not afraid to lose your voice.

Worship like you're not afraid of losing yourself.

Preach like the end of the world is tomorrow.

You are a child of God, so

Forgive as you've been forgiven much.

Obey when he calls you to the daily feast of his Word.

Love and keep loving, give and keep giving, forgive and keep

forgiving.

Acknowledgments

To my Lord and Savior, Jesus Christ: I am humbled to be your servant. You transformed my life and renewed my heart. When I was lost, you found me. When I was broken, you healed my wounds. You put a new song in my spirit. I owe you my life. This book is yours, Lord. I dedicate it to you. May your light shine through its words. May your truth heal and revive the hurting soul—as it did mine.

I want to thank my editor, Ambria Florence, for her exceptional work on this project. She gave honest feedback and held nothing back when challenging sneaky unbiblical beliefs. Like many Christians, I had unconsciously accepted certain secular doctrines as truth, when in reality they contradict the Bible. The process of weeding out misconceptions and making major revisions was a humbling experience. I had no idea editing would inspire such growth in my faith and understanding of Scripture. Ambria has helped me become a better writer.

I want to thank my mom, Lucy Muya, for encouraging me to write this book. She was a faithful follower and champion of the devotional series I posted on Facebook, 40Before40. Encouraged by my messages, she asked me to publish a full book. My mom is highly ambitious—she thinks big! Thank you for believing in me even more than I believe in myself.

Thank you to my dad, Charles Muya, for exhorting me to move forward and never look back. You advised me to focus, settle down, and reclaim control of my finances. You taught me many lessons about investing in my future. Now I see why leaving a legacy is important. This book is one of those legacies.

Josiah, my dear son, you are too young to know the immeasurable impact you have made on me. I don't know where I'd be if you hadn't been born. You changed my life. You gave me a reason to wake up early every day and work to finish this project. Thank you for being so patient with me through this process. There were times you had to entertain yourself while I typed away at the computer. Now that this book is done, we will spend more time together.

To the rest of the family (Thomas, Wanjiru, Naomi, Duncan, Susan, and Pastor Jane), thank you. You truly are the pillars in my life, the core support that is always there, through thick and thin. Thank you for standing by me when times were rough, as they often were. God created family as a safety net, an entourage through adversity. You have exemplified his design. We have faced a season of suffering since Faith passed away in January. As an added blow, the COVID-19 pandemic has prevented our gathering as a family. Yet I believe that God is doing a great work in our hearts, refining us so we will never be the same again. I pray you will find encouragement within the pages of this book as we continue to heal from our loss.

Thank you, Andiswa Madolwana, for turning the tables and becoming my volunteer life coach. I began as your life coach, but when the enemy came swinging, you stepped up and coached me through the most difficult season of my life. You poured so much wisdom into me, and I will always be grateful for the many hours we spent encouraging one another in the faith. My passion for discipleship comes from the transformation it brought us. This is what Jesus meant when he said to go into the world and make disciples of all nations (Matthew 28:18-20).

Thank you, Anne Stinnette, for reading through my first draft and kickstarting the editing process. I knew the technical work would prove the hardest part of self-publishing, so I am grateful to have had the counsel of a seasoned Bible scholar and mature believer. The editing process was, in itself, a season of spiritual formation. Theological accuracy is vital to a sound Christian book, so thank you for sharing your insight and for proofreading my manuscript.

To my Ephesians Girls (Frances, Anne, Betsy, and Mary), thank you. How blessed I am to have such a faithful group of friends. I have grown by leaps and bounds since first welcoming you into my life nine years ago. We spent many hours digging deep into God's Word at the lobby of Westin Hotel. It was through our meetings that I developed the hunger to read and apply Scripture daily. You sparked my desire to share truth with others on a one-on-one level.

I want to thank Reverend Mack Brandon for examining my doctrinal claims and keeping me true to the Bible. I am grateful for the time you spent showing me where to improve my writing. Correcting both content and grammar, you mentored me through the writing process and helped shape my message. Thank you for your wisdom, leadership, and friendship.

Thank you, Grace Gateere, for helping with the editing process. We have known each other since high school, and I am forever grateful for our time-tested friendship.

To the Bower Family (Pastor Jeff, Michelle, Aaron, Abigail, and Joshua), thank you. Your support and faithful presence during the darkest season of my life mean the world to me. You demonstrated God's love through your wonderful hospitality.

Thank you, Rick Davis, for your constant love, support, and availability. I am so grateful for your willingness to listen whenever I needed to vent out my frustrations. A friend in need is a friend indeed. I cannot thank you enough for all you do for me and Josiah.

I want to thank my aunt Nancy Gichimu for believing in me. You showed me I could have a better life and opened my eyes to the abundance God promises. You took me in and planted my feet for a fresh start. I will be forever grateful for your generosity.

Last but not least, thank you to my Church family at Agape SLO, Rock Harbor Christian Fellowship, and CITAM.

About the Author

Julz was born and raised in Nairobi, Kenya. She is a certified life coach who empowers women to embrace their identity in Christ so they can move on from past hurts and live joyful, fulfilled lives. Since experiencing the radical restoration of her own soul, she has made it her mission to champion the healing woman, exhorting Christians to root their spiritual foundations in the truth and freedom of God's Word.

She has a Bachelor's degree in Communication and a Master teacher Certificate in Early Childhood Development and Education. She also studied theology and music in a worship leadership program at Azusa Pacific University.

Julz is an activist, raising awareness of the harmful effects of orphanages in Kenya. She urges people to remember that, together, we can ensure that each child has the opportunity to grow up in a safe, loving family.

She enjoys playing piano and guitar, singing and songwriting.

Contact Julz Muya

Website: www.mymentor.life/juliamuya

Email: julzmuya@gmail.com

Facebook: www.facebook.com/julzmuya

Instagram: @julzmuya

Made in United States
Orlando, FL
10 June 2024